Student's Book 1

On Your Way

Building Basic Skills in English

Larry Anger

Cheryl Pavlik

Margaret Keenan Segal

Longman

Executive Editor: Joanne Dresner
Development Editor: Nancy Perry
Production Editor: Catherine Hulbert
Book Design: Lynn Luchetti
Cover Illustration: Bill Schmidt
Production Director: Eduardo Castillo
Permissions and Photo Research: Esther Gottfried, Robert Kellerman
Photo Credits: See page 122.

Review Sections by Marjorie Fuchs

We wish to thank the following artists:
Storyline artist: Melodye Rosales.
Interior artists: Beth J. Baum, Marie DeJohn, Kathie Kelleher, Joseph Maslan, Claudia Karabaic Sargent, Roman Szolkowski, Nina Tallarico, Phyllis Tarlow.

On Your Way   Student's Book 1

Copyright © 1987 by Longman Inc.

ISBN: 0–582–90760–8

Longman Inc.
95 Church St.
White Plains, N.Y. 10601

Associated companies:
Longman Group Ltd., London; Longman Cheshire Pty., Melbourne; Longman Paul Pty., Auckland; Copp Clark Pitman, Toronto; Pitman Publishing Inc., New York

Library of Congress Cataloging-in-Publication Data
Anger, Larry, 1942-
  On your way.

  Includes index.
  1. English language—Text-books for foreign speakers.
I. Pavlik, Cheryl, 1949-   . II. Segal, Margaret,
1950-   . III. Title.
PE1128.A53   1986   428.2′4   86-21524
ISBN 0-582-90760-8 (v. 1)

      89 90 9 8 7 6 5 4

Distributed in the United Kingdom by Longman Group Ltd., Longman House, Burnt Mill, Harlow, Essex CM20 2JE, England, and by associated companies, branches, and representatives throughout the world.

Printed in the U.S.A.

Consultants

JOSEPH BERKOWITZ
ESOL Program Coordinator
Miami Sunset Adult Education Center
Dade County
Miami, Florida

EILEEN K. BLAU
Associate Professor
Department of English
University of Puerto Rico
Mayaguez, Puerto Rico

CHERYL CREATORE
Curriculum Coordinator of ESL
Seneca Community College
Toronto, Ontario, Canada

JUDITH E. KLEEMAN
Manager Refugee Program
Houston Community College
Houston, Texas

JOANN LA PERLA
Director of Continuing Education and
    Community Services
Union County College
Cranford, New Jersey

VIRGINIA LOCASTRO
Lecturer
The University of Tsukuba
Japan

BARBARA MOTEN
Assistant Director – Project C3
Department of Adult Education
Detroit Public Schools
Detroit, Michigan

K. LYNN SAVAGE
Vocational ESL Resource Instructor
San Francisco Community College Centers
San Francisco, California

Contents

1 Listen.

1 Hi. My name's Ron Wolinski. I'm from Houston.

2 Hi. My name's Marty Cruz. I'm from Los Angeles.

3 Hello. My name's Chris McCann. I'm from San Francisco.

4 And I'm Jim McCann. I'm from San Francisco too.

2 Match the name with the city.

Name		City
1. _C_	Ron	**a.** San Francisco
2. ____	Chris	**b.** Los Angeles
3. ____	Jim	**c.** Houston
4. ____	Marty	

3 Warm Up

Introduce yourself.

Hi. My name's . . . I'm from . . . (too).

DEVELOP YOUR VOCABULARY

Hello.
Good morning.
. . .

1

Practice

A.

I	am 'm	
You We They	are 're	from Los Angeles.
He She It	is 's	

I am	=	I'm
you are	=	you're
we are	=	we're
they are	=	they're
he is	=	he's
she is	=	she's
it is	=	it's

1 Where are they from? Complete the sentences with *I'm, He's, She's, They're* or *We're*.

1. *We're* from China.

2. *They're* from Laos.

3. _____ from Mexico.

4. _____ from Poland.

5. _____ from Japan.

6. _____ from Vietnam.

7. _____ from Canada.

8. What about you?

_____ from . . .

For names of other countries, see page 116.

2 Where are these things from? Complete the sentences with *It's* or *They're*.

1. *It's* from Germany.   2. _____ from China.   3. _____ from Japan.   4. _____ from Greece.

B.

I	am 'm	
You We They	are 're	**not** from Los Angeles.
He She It	is 's	

Correct a classmate.

1. A: He's from Los Angeles.
   B: No, *he's* not from *Los Angeles. He's* from *Houston.*
   A: Oh, that's right.
2. She's from San Francisco.
3. It's from the United States.
4. They're from Houston.
5. They're from Poland.

1   2

3   4   5

C.

What's your name?	My name's Ron.
Where are you from?	I'm from Houston.
Where's Houston?	It's in Texas.

1 **Look at the map. Find Phoenix, Houston, Los Angeles, San Francisco, Seattle, New York City, Chicago, Denver, Miami, Toronto and Montreal.**

A: Where's *San Francisco?*
B: It's in *California.*
A: Where's *California?*
B: It's right here. And *San Francisco* is right here.

2 **What's your name and where are you from? Point to the country on the map.**

A: What's your name?
B: My name's *Luc.*
A: Where are you from?
B: I'm from *Canada.*
A: Where's that?
B: It's right here.

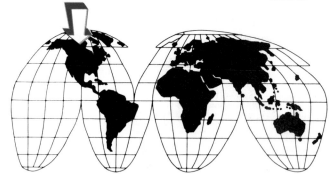

3 **Listen to the conversation and complete it.**

RON: *Hi*___. My ___ Ron. What's ___ name?
     1   2   3

TED: ___ ___ Ted.
     4   5

RON: ___ are you ___?
     6   7

TED: ___ from Seattle. What about ___?
     8   9

RON: I'm ___ Houston.
       10

Now practice the conversation with a classmate. Talk about yourself.

Life Skills

The Alphabet • Spelling

1 Say the alphabet.

the printed alphabet

A a B b C c D d E e F f G g H h I i

J j K k L l M m N n O o P p Q q

R r S s T t U u V v W w X x Y y Z z

the written alphabet

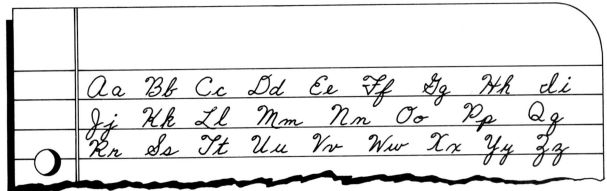

2 Say these letters.

1. a j k h
2. e b c d g p t v z
3. i y
4. o u q w
5. f l m n s x
6. r

3 Listen and choose the correct letter.

1. (a) e   6. i (y)
2. j (g)   7. (o) u
3. a (h)   8. (y) i
4. (e) i   9. (m) n
5. c (s)

4 Spell the names.

1. Ron Wolinski
2. *Ted Lyons*
3. *Marty Cruz*
4. *Jim McCann*
5. Chris McCann
6. _____
   (your name)

5 Say your last name and spell it.

A: What's your last name?
B: *Lyons.*
A: How do you spell that?
B: *L-y-o-n-s.*

Just for Fun

6 Complete the chart.

Country	Nationality
China	Chinese
————	Japanese
————	Mexican
————	Laotian
————	Polish
————	Canadian
————	Vietnamese

Where are you from? . . . What's your nationality? . . .

For other countries and nationalities, see page 116.

---

7 Look at the example. Then print and sign your name.

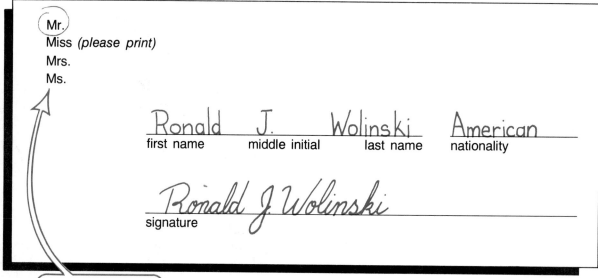

Mr.
Miss *(please print)*
Mrs.
Ms.

Ronald   J.   Wolinski   American
first name   middle initial   last name   nationality

Ronald J. Wolinski
signature

Ms. = Miss or Mrs.

Mr.
Miss *(please print)*
Mrs.
Ms.

first name   middle initial   last name   nationality

signature

For Your Information

Classroom instructions

Follow the instructions.

Please open your book to page 6.
Read the instructions.
Now close your book.
Take out a piece of paper.
Print your name on your paper.
   Don't sign your name. Print your name.
Now sign your name.
Please give me your paper.

Note: Imperative	
Affirmative	**Negative**
Write your name.	**Don't write** your name.
Open your book.	**Don't open** your book.
Look at your book.	**Don't look** at your book.

8 Listen to the conversations and choose the correct last name of each passenger.

1. Beth   a. _____ Gramer
             b. __✓__ Kramer

2. Andrew   a. _____ Murray
             b. _____ Murphy

3. Ed   a. _____ Taylor
             b. _____ Thayer

4. Lucille   a. _____ Rollins
             b. _____ Roland

5. Ellen   a. _____ Quon
             b. _____ Kwon

For pronunciation exercises for Unit 1, see page 109.

2 Nice to Meet You

1 Marty, Chris and Jim are on vacation. They're in Phoenix now. Ron is in Phoenix too. Listen to their conversation.

1

RON: Hi. How are you today?
MARTY: Fine, thanks. And you?
RON: Not too bad.

2

RON: Where are you going?
MARTY: We're going to Los Angeles.
RON: Oh, I'm going to L.A. too.

3

RON: My name's Ron.
MARTY: Hi. I'm Marty.
RON: Marty?
MARTY: Yeah. My name's Marta. My nickname's Marty.
RON: Oh.

4

MARTY: Ron, this is my sister Chris.
CHRIS: Hi.
MARTY: And this is her husband, Jim.
JIM: Hi. It's nice to meet you.
RON: Nice to meet you too.

2 Choose the correct response.

1. _d_ How are you?
2. ____ Ron, this is my sister Chris.
3. ____ It's nice to meet you.
4. ____ Where are you going?

a. Nice to meet you too.
b. I'm going to Los Angeles.
c. Hi. It's nice to meet you.
d. Fine, thanks.

3 Warm Up

Greet a classmate.

A: *Hi. How are you?*
B: *Fine, thanks. And you?*
A: *Not too bad.*

DEVELOP YOUR VOCABULARY

pretty good
OK
. . .

─Practice─

A.

My	name's Jim.	I'm from San Francisco.
Our	names are Jim and Chris McCann.	We're from San Francisco.
His	name's Ron.	He's from Houston.
Her	name's Chris.	She's from San Francisco.
Their	last name's Santos.	They're from Phoenix.

1   Ask Chris about her family. Complete the conversation with *my, your, his, her, our* and *their*.

YOU: What's _*your*_ last name?
     ₁

CHRIS: _____ last name's McCann. We're
     ₂
from San Francisco.

YOU: And what's _____ name?
     ₃

CHRIS: _____ name's Jim. He's my husband.
     ₄

YOU: What's _____ name?
     ₅

CHRIS: _____ name's Marty. She's from L.A.
     ₆
She's my sister.

YOU: And what's _____ last name?
     ₇

CHRIS: _____ last name's Santos. Grandma
     ₈
and Grandpa Santos are from Phoenix.

What's _____ name?
     ₉

YOU: _____ name's . . . I'm from . . .
     ₁₀

2   Ask about your classmates.

A. What's his (her) name?
B: His (Her) name's . . .
    OR   I can't remember.
A: Where's he (she) from?
B: He's (She's) from . . .
    OR   I can't remember.

B.

singular

| **This** is my brother Alan, **and this** is my brother Steve. |
| **These** are my brothers, Alan **and** Steve. |

plural

1 Introduce two people.

A: *Ron*, this is *Chris*.
B: (It's) Nice to meet you.
C: (It's) Nice to meet you too.

2 Identify the people in the pictures. Use *This is* or *These are*.

```
Mr. Wolinski————————————Mrs. Wolinski

Steve      Alan      Ron     Barbara⌐Jack Kelly
                                  ⌐      ⌐
                              Sarah      Sue
```

1

2

3

4

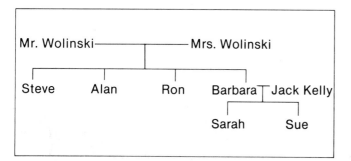

1. *This is* Ron.
2. _____ _____ his parents.
3. _____ _____ his brother Alan.
4. _____ _____ his brother Steve.
5. _____ _____ his sister, Barbara, and her husband, Jack.
6. _____ _____ their children, Sarah and Sue.

5

6

3 Say the singular or the plural of these words.

Singular	**Plural**
his brother	his *brothers*
our _____	our sisters
my friend	my _____
her _____	her classmates

This word is different:

| their child | their _____ |

4 Tell about your family.

A: Are you married?
B: Yes, I am.   OR   No, I'm not.
A: Do you have any children?
B: Yes, I have *a son and a daughter.*
   OR   No, I don't.

DEVELOP YOUR VOCABULARY

a son	a boy
two daughters	two girls
three sons	three boys
four daughters	four girls
. . .	. . .

5 Show photos of your family or friends.

This is my *husband, Jack,* and these are my
children, Sarah and Sue.

**For other members of the family,
see page 114.**

DEVELOP YOUR VOCABULARY

husband	father	boyfriend
wife	mother	girlfriend
	fiancé	. . .
	fiancée	. . .

6 Learn about Ellen Quon and her family. Listen and complete the paragraph.

Our last _____ Quon. _____ name's
 1   2   3
Ellen, and this is _____ husband, Richard.
                    4
_____ are _in_ Los Angeles. These _____
 5   6   7
our children. This _____ our daughter,
                    8
Maxine, with her dog, Skip. And this is
_____ son, Henry. _____ nickname's Hank.
 9   10
_____ are my parents. _____ last name's
 11   12
Wang. _____ from Hong Kong.
       13

Ellen   Richard   Maxine   Henry
Chu Wang   Mai Wang   Skip

Just for Fun

7 Complete the chart with nicknames from Unit 1 and Unit 2.

Name	Nickname
Henry	*Hank*
Ronald	_____
Marta	_____
Christina	_____
James	_____
Steven	_____
Susan	_____

Do you have a nickname? What is it? . . .

C.

Where **are**	you they	going?	I	'm	**going** to Los Angeles. **not going** anywhere.
			We They	're	
Where**'s**	he she it		He She It	's	

Spelling note

verb + *ing*

go ⟶ going

1 Where are they from? Where are they going?

1. A: Where'*s she* from?
   B: *She's* from *Chicago.*
   A: Where'*s she* going?
   B: *She's* going to *Denver*.

1

2

3

4

5

6

2 Look at the pictures. Ask questions with *what* and answer them. Then write your questions and give them to a classmate. Your classmate will write the answers.

1. A: What's Clara doing?
   B: She's reading a magazine.

1. Clara/read a magazine

2. Miguel/write a letter

3. Bob/listen to a cassette

4. Kathy and Ed/look at a map

5. Maria and Alice do their homework

6. the people/wait for a bus

> **Spelling note**
> writé + ing ⟶ writing
> get + t + ing ⟶ getting

3 Pretend you are talking on the telephone.

A: Hello?
B: Hi, *Steve*. This is *Alan*.
A: Oh, hi.
B: What are you doing?
A: I'm *reading a letter*.

> ### DEVELOP YOUR VOCABULARY
>
> I'm watching TV.
> I'm cleaning the house.
> I'm not doing anything right now.
> . . .

4 Dictation

Beth Kramer is on vacation. She is flying to Los Angeles. Listen to the conversation. Then listen again and complete it.

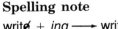

BETH: My name's Beth Kramer.
ELLEN: I'm Ellen Quon. _This is my husband, Richard_ .
                                                    1
RICHARD: Nice to meet you.
BETH: _____ ?
                    2
ELLEN: We're going to Los Angeles. We're from L.A. What about you?
BETH: _____ .
                    3
RICHARD: Where are you from?
BETH: _____ .
                    4

Now pretend you are on vacation. Practice the conversation with two classmates. Talk about yourself.

Life Skills

Numbers 0 to 9

1 Say the numbers. Then count from zero to nine.

0	1	2	3	4	5	6	7	8	9
zero	one	two	three	four	five	six	seven	eight	nine

2 Read the license plate numbers.

1

2

3

4

5

6

7

8

3 Listen to the conversation and write each license plate number.

1. California license plate number 5 D Y K 1 4 6
2. Nevada license plate number __ __ __ __ __ __ __
3. Arizona license plate number __ __ __ __ __ __ __
4. Arizona license plate number __ __ __ __ __ __ __

For Your Information

Classroom expressions

I don't know.
I don't feel well.
I'm sorry I'm late.
I don't understand.
I forgot my homework.
Would you repeat that, please?

Now choose the best classroom expression for each picture.

ON YOUR OWN
Do one of the following:

1 **Roleplay:** Turn to the conversation on page 8. Pretend you are waiting for a bus or a plane. Practice the conversation.

2 **Improvise:** Work with three classmates. Change the conversation on page 8. Add your own information. Then present your conversation to the class.

For pronunciation exercises for Unit 2, see page 109.

REVIEW 1

1   Rewrite these sentences using *I, you, we, they, he, she* and *it*.

1. Chris, where are *you and Jim* going?

Chris, where are *you* going?

2. *Jim and I* are going back to San Francisco.
3. And your sister? Where's *your sister* going?
4. *My sister* is going to Los Angeles.

5. And her friend Ron? Where's *Ron* going?
6. *Ron's* going to L.A. too.
7. Where's *Ron* from?
8. Houston. *Houston's* in Texas.

2   Complete these sentences with *am, is* or *are*.

My name ___*is*___ Ron Wolinski. I _____ going to Los Angeles. I _____ from
Texas. My parents _____ in Houston. My brother Al _____ in Dallas. My brother
Steve _____ in Dallas too. Al and Steve _____ studying there. My sister, Barbara,
and her family _____ in San Antonio.

3   Rewrite each sentence using a contraction. Look at the example.

1. What is your name?

What's your name?

2. My name is Ron Wolinski. I am from
   Houston, and I am going to Los Angeles.
3. Where is Los Angeles?
4. It is in California.

5. And your friend Marty? Where is she
   going?
6. Marty is going to Los Angeles too. She is
   from there.
7. And what is their name?
8. Their name is McCann. They are from San
   Francisco.

4   Correct these sentences. Use the word in parentheses.

1. Marty and Ron are in New York. (Phoenix)

They're not in New York. They're in Phoenix.

2. They're waiting for a plane. (bus)
3. They're going to Houston. (Los Angeles)

4. Los Angeles is in Texas. (California)
5. Chris is going back to Seattle. (San
   Francisco)
6. Chris and her husband are from Seattle.
   (San Francisco)

Now correct these sentences. Use your own information.

1. I'm from the United States.

2. I'm studying Chinese here.

5   Complete these sentences with *this is* or *these are*.

My name's Barbara Wolinski Kelly. ___*This is*___ my husband, Jack, and
_____ our children, Sarah and Sue. _____ my parents. _____ my
brother Ron, and _____ my brothers Al and Steve.

6   Complete the chart with singular and plural words.

Singular	Plural	Singular	Plural
my sister	my *sisters*	her child	her _____
our _____	our friends	their _____	their brothers
his son	his _____	our _____	our classmates

16

7 Learn about Ellen Quon and her family. Complete these sentences with *my, your, our, his, her* or *their.*

1. _Our_ last name's Quon. We're from Los Angeles.

2. _____ name's Ellen, and this is _____ husband, Richard.

3. I have a son. _____ name's Henry.

4. I have a daughter too. _____ name's Maxine.

5. _____ parents are in Los Angeles now too. They're from Hong Kong. _____ last name is Wang.

8 Write questions using *What* and *Where* and answer them.

1. A: What are you reading?
   B: I'm reading a magazine.
2. A: _____ ?
   B: They're going to Los Angeles.
3. A: _____ ?
   B: We're going back to New York.
4. A: _____ ?
   B: I'm doing my homework.

9 Complete these questions. Then answer them with your own information.

1. A: _What_'s your name?
   B: _____ .
2. A: _____ are you from?
   B: _____ .
                (your city)
3. A: _____'s that?
   B: _____ .
                (your country)

10 Match the sentences in column A with the responses in column B.

A	B
1. _f_ How are you?	a. Quon.
2. ___ What's your last name, Ellen?	b. I'm reading my English book.
3. ___ How do you spell that?	c. Yes, I have a son and a daughter.
4. ___ It's nice to meet you.	d. Q-U-O-N.
5. ___ What are you doing?	e. Nice to meet you.
6. ___ Are you married?	f. Pretty good.
7. ___ This is my husband, Jim.	g. Yes, I am.
8. ___ Do you have any children?	h. Nice to meet you too.

Just for Fun

11 Make sentences with these words.

1. book your Don't look at .
Don't look at your book.

2. understand I don't .
3. his What's name ?

4. Where's from she ?
5. looking at They're homework their .
6. is my This boyfriend .

12 Complete this form with your own information.

Name _____

Nationality _____

Father's name _____ Mother's name _____

Number of sisters _____ Number of brothers _____

Married ____ yes ____ no *Spouse's name _____

Children ____ yes ____ no Number of children _____

*spouse = husband or wife

3 Are You All From San Francisco?

1 Chris and Jim are talking to a passenger. Listen to their conversation.

1

CHRIS: Oh, the bus is ready.
PASSENGER: What time is it?
JIM: It's six o'clock.
PASSENGER: Oh, it's late.

2

JIM: It's very late. And I'm tired and hungry.
CHRIS: Yeah. And Mom and Dad are waiting at the bus station.

3

PASSENGER: Where are you from?
CHRIS: San Francisco.
PASSENGER: Are you all from San Francisco?
CHRIS: No, we aren't. My sister is from L.A. And her friend is from Houston.

4

PASSENGER: Are you going back to San Francisco today?
JIM: No, we aren't. We're staying in L.A. tonight, and we're going back to San Francisco tomorrow.

2 Say *That's right, That's wrong* or *I don't know.*

1. It's four o'clock.
2. Chris's parents are waiting at the bus station.
3. The passenger is from Phoenix.
4. Chris, Jim, Marty and Ron are all from Phoenix.
5. Chris and Jim are going back to San Francisco tonight.

3 Warm Up

Do you remember where a classmate is from? Ask him or her.

A: Are you from . . .?
B: Yes, I am.
   OR
A: Are you from . . .?
B: No, I'm not. I'm from . . .
A: Oh, that's right.

18

Practice

A.

Am	I			you	are.		you	aren't.
				I	am.		I	'm not.
Are	you they	on the bus? at the bus station? going to Los Angeles?	Yes,	we they	are.	No,	we they	aren't.
Is	he she it			he she it	is.		he she it	isn't.

are not	=	're not	OR	aren't
is not	=	's not	OR	isn't

Just for Fun

1 Find a classmate and introduce yourself.

A: Excuse me, are you   OR
   Toshi Ogawa?

B: No, I'm not.

A: Oh, sorry.

A: Excuse me, are you
   Toshi Ogawa?

B: Yes, I am.

A: Oh, good. I'm *Carlos Ortega.*

2 Marty's parents, Elena and Herman García, and her son, Jeff, are at the L.A. bus station. Look at the picture. Then ask and answer questions.

1. Mr. and Mrs. García/be at the bus station

A: Are Mr. and Mrs. García at the bus station?

B: Yes, they are.

2. Mr. García/read a newspaper
3. Mrs. García/read a newspaper
4. Jeff/sleep

5. they all/wait for the bus
6. the bus/be from San Francisco
7. the bus/be from Phoenix
8. Marty, Chris, Jim and Ron/be on the bus
9. the Garcías/wait for Marty, Chris and Jim
10. they/wait for Ron

3 Marty is talking to a passenger on the bus. Listen and complete their conversation.

PASSENGER: Are _you_ from Chicago?
                    1

MARTY: No, _____ not. I'm _____ Los Angeles.
                      2   3

PASSENGER: Are you _____ to Chicago?
                        4

MARTY: No, I'm _____. I'm going back _____ L.A.
                        5   6

PASSENGER: Back to L.A.? Is this bus going to Los Angeles?

MARTY: Yes, _____ is.
                    7

PASSENGER: Oh, no! I'm _____ the wrong bus!
                          8

B.

We're staying in Los Angeles We're going back to San Francisco	tonight. tomorrow. next week/weekend. on Sunday.

1 Say the days of the week. Then ask and answer these questions:

A: What day is today?
B: It's *Tuesday.*
A: What day is tomorrow?
B: It's *Wednesday.*

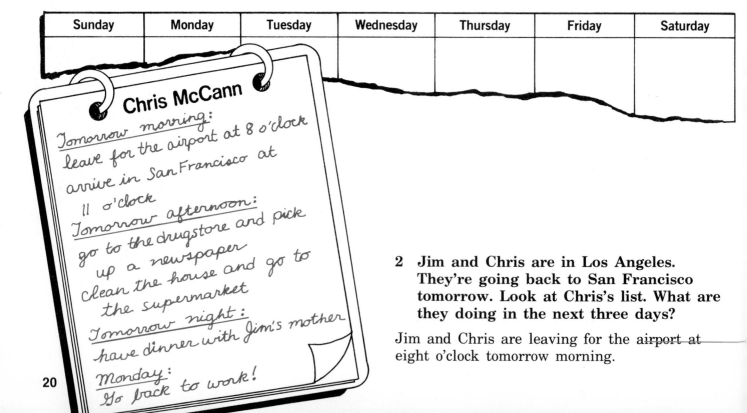

Sunday	Monday	Tuesday	Wednesday	Thursday	Friday	Saturday

Chris McCann

Tomorrow morning:
leave for the airport at 8 o'clock
arrive in San Francisco at 11 o'clock
Tomorrow afternoon:
go to the drugstore and pick up a newspaper
clean the house and go to the supermarket
Tomorrow night:
have dinner with Jim's mother
Monday:
Go back to work!

2 Jim and Chris are in Los Angeles. They're going back to San Francisco tomorrow. Look at Chris's list. What are they doing in the next three days?

Jim and Chris are leaving for the airport at eight o'clock tomorrow morning.

3 Ask a classmate what he or she is doing tonight, tomorrow or next weekend.

A: What are you doing *next weekend?*
B: I'm *working on Saturday,* and I'm *going to the beach on Sunday.* What are you doing?
A: I'm *not doing anything special.*

come to school	go to a movie
go shopping	clean the house
go dancing	. . .

C.

Is she	early,	or	is she	late?	She's early.
Are they			are they		They're late.

1 Look at the pictures. Complete each sentence with the correct word.

1. They're _early_ .
    early/late

2. He's _____ .
    early/late

3. She's _____ .
    tired/sick

4. They're _____ .
    hungry/thirsty

5. He's _____ .
    hungry/thirsty

6. She's _____ .
    sad/happy

7. They're _____ .
    sad/happy

8. She's _____ .
    sick/tired

2 Find out about the people in Exercise 1.

1. A: Are they early, or are they late?
    B: They're early.

3 Pretend you are on an airplane. Ask and answer questions like this:

1. FLIGHT ATTENDANT: Are you thirsty?
    PASSENGER: Yes, I am.   OR   No, I'm not.

4 Ellen Quon and her husband, Richard, are at Los Angeles International Airport. Listen and complete the conversation.

MR. GREEN: Excuse _me_ . Are _____ Ms. Quon?
                          1   2

WOMAN: No, _____ not.
                      3

MR. GREEN: Oh, sorry. _____ me. _____ you
                            4   5
            Ms. Quon?

ELLEN: Yes, _____ _____ .
                       6   7

MR. GREEN: Oh, _good_ . My _____ Marty
                      8   9
            Green. I'm from the Beverly Limousine
            Service.

ELLEN: Oh, yes.

MR. GREEN: _____ your _____ with you,
                 10   11
            Ms. Quon?

ELLEN: Yes, _____ _____ . He's _____ here.
                      12   13   14

Now practice the conversation with two classmates. Use your own names.

— Life Skills

Numbers 10 to 1,000 • Telling time

1 Say the numbers.

10 ten	**11** eleven	**12** twelve	**13** thirteen	**14** fourteen
15 fifteen	**16** sixteen	**17** seventeen	**18** eighteen	**19** nineteen
20 twenty	**21** twenty-one	**22** twenty-two	**23** twenty-three	**24** twenty-four
25 twenty-five	**26** twenty-six	**27** twenty-seven	**28** twenty-eight	**29** twenty-nine
30 thirty	**40** forty	**50** fifty	**60** sixty	**70** seventy
80 eighty	**90** ninety	**100** one hundred OR a hundred	**1,000** one thousand OR a thousand	

2 Say these numbers.

1. 12   20
2. 13   30
3. 14   40
4. 15   50
5. 16   60
6. 17   70
7. 18   80
8. 19   90

3 Listen and choose the correct number.

1. 15   (50)
2. 30   (13)
3. (14)   40
4. (17)   70
5. 60   (16)
6. (40)   14
7. 13   (30)
8. 50   (15)

Just for Fun

4 Practice counting.

1. Count from 1 to 20.
   1, 2, 3 . . .
2. Count backward from 20 to 10.
   20, 19, 18 . . .
3. Count to 50 by 5's.
   5, 10, 15 . . .
4. Count to 150 by 10's.
   10, 20, 30 . . .

5 What time is it?

1. It's 5:00.
   (It's five o'clock.)

2. It's 5:05.
   (It's five-oh-five.)

3. It's 5:15.
   (It's five fifteen.)

4. It's 5:30.
   (It's five thirty.)

6 Listen to the conversations and write the time.

1. _3:00_
2. _____
3. _____
4. _____
5. _____
6. _____

7 Ask a classmate for the time.

A: Excuse me. What time is it, please?   OR   A: Excuse me. What time is it, please?
B: It's *8:35*.   B: I'm sorry, I don't have a watch.
A: Thank you very much.   A: OK, thanks anyway.

24

For Your Information

Ways to tell time

You can say:

1 It's five fifteen. OR It's a quarter after five.

2 It's five thirty. OR It's half past five.

3 It's five forty-five. OR It's a quarter to six.

Say the time two ways.

4    **5**    **6**

8 Dictation

Beth Kramer is at Los Angeles International Airport. She's waiting for a bus. Listen to the conversation. Then listen again and complete it.

BETH: _____1_____?

WOMAN: _____2_____.

BETH: _____3_____.

WOMAN: _____4_____?

BETH: _____5_____.

WOMAN: Well, the bus is over there.
BETH: Oh, thank you.

ON YOUR OWN
Do one of the following:

1 Roleplay: Turn to the conversation on page 18. Pretend you and a friend are talking to someone on a bus, train or plane. Practice the conversation.

2 Improvise: Work with two classmates. Change the conversation on page 18. Add your own information. Then present your conversation to the class.

For pronunciation exercises for Unit 3, see page 110.

UNIT 4 What's That?

1 Everyone is at Ron's hotel. Listen to their conversation.

1

RON: Well, thanks for the ride.

MARTY: You're welcome. Can I help you with your things?

RON: No, that's OK. Thanks.

2

JEFF: Whose magazine is this?

RON: Oh, it's mine.

JEFF: Is this your pen too?

RON: Yeah. Thanks, Jeff.

3

JEFF: What's that?

RON: A guitar.

JEFF: Can you play?

RON: Yes, but not very well.

4

RON: Well, goodbye. Thanks again.

MARTY: Bye. I'll see you soon.

RON: Oh, wait a minute. What's your telephone number?

MARTY: Oh, it's 924−3076.

2 Say *That's right, That's wrong* or *It doesn't say*.

1. Ron is at his hotel.
2. Ron can play the guitar.
3. Marty can play the guitar very well.
4. The telephone number at the hotel is 924−3076.

3 Warm Up

Find the owners of things in the classroom. Use *this* or *these*.

A: (Excuse me.) Is this your *magazine?*

B: Yes, it is. Thank you.

A: You're welcome.

A: (Excuse me.) Are these your *books?*

B: No, they aren't.

DEVELOP YOUR VOCABULARY

bag	money	pen
backpack	keys	pencil
notebook	. . .	. . .

Practice

A.

What's	this? **that?**	It's	**a** guitar. **an** umbrella.
What are	these? **those?**	They're	guitars. umbrellas.

this   that   these   those

Use *a* before consonants.

a guitar
a cassette player
a magazine
a hat
a piece of chalk

Use *an* before vowel sounds (a, e, i, o, u).

an apple
an eraser
an identification card (ID card)
an orange
an umbrella

1 Identify things in the classroom.

A: What's this (that)?
B: It's a (an) . . .
A: What are these (those)?
B: They're . . .

2 Marty is bringing presents from Phoenix for her family. Ask Marty about the presents.

YOU: What's that?
MARTY: It's a *wallet* for my *dad*.
YOU: Oh, that's nice. What color is it?
MARTY: It's *brown*.

See p. 114 for a list of colors.

This is what is in the boxes:

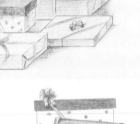

1. wallet

2. sweater

3. purse

4. blouse

5. shirt

6. jacket

B.

Whose	magazine is this? bag is that? car keys are these? things are those?	**That** magazine is **mine.** **This** bag is **yours.** **Those** keys are Mr. and Mrs. García**'s.** **These** things are Marty**'s.**

1 Identify the owners of things in the classroom.

A: *This pen* is *mine.*
B: *Those books* are *the teacher's.*
C: . . .

2 Say something is yours.

A: Excuse me. *That pen* is mine.
B: Oh, sorry.
A: That's OK.

3 Find the owners.

A: Whose *hat* is *this?*
B: It's *Ron's.*
　 OR I think it's *yours.*
　 OR I don't know.
A: Whose things are *those?*
B: They're *mine.*
　 OR I think they're *Ron's.*
　 OR I don't know.

DEVELOP YOUR VOCABULARY

gloves　　　　　　　　scarf

coat　　　　　　　　. . .

4 Beth is at the Plaza Hotel. Listen and complete the conversation.

BELLMAN: *Are* these bags _____?
　　　　　1　　　　　　　2
BETH:　　Yes, _____ are.
　　　　　　　　3
BELLMAN: _____ else?
　　　　　4
BETH:　　_____, that's _____.
　　　　　5　　　　　6
BELLMAN: _____ tennis racket is _____?
　　　　　7　　　　　　　　8
BETH:　　Oh, I'm sorry. That's _____ too.
　　　　　　　　　　　　　9
BELLMAN: Is _____ all?
　　　　　　10
BETH:　　Yes. _____ for your help.
　　　　　　　11
BELLMAN: You're welcome.

Now pretend you are at a hotel. Practice the conversation with a classmate.

C.

I You He She (It) We They	**can** **cannot** **can't**	play the guitar. swim.

Can you	play the guitar? swim?	Yes, I **can**. No, I **can't**.

cannot (one word) = **can't**

1 Talk about the pictures.

1a. Susan can play softball.
1b. Susan can't swim.
2. . . .

2 What can the people in Exercise 1 do?

1a. A: Can Susan play softball?
    B: Yes, she can.

1b. A: Can she swim?
    B: No, she can't.

1a. Susan/play softball

1b. Susan/swim

2a. Toshi/play football

2b. Toshi/play tennis

3a. Hua and Joe
    play soccer

3b. Hua and Joe/ski

4a. Maria and Luis
    roller skate

4b. Maria and Luis
    ice skate

3 Look at the sentences. Then talk about yourself.

Susan can play softball, **but** she can't swim. Susan can't swim, **but** she can play softball.

4 Look at the pictures in Exercise 1 again. Then talk and write about the people like this:

1. Susan can play softball, but she can't swim.
2. Toshi can't play football, but he can play tennis.
3. . . .

Note: Put a comma (,) before *but*.

29

Just for Fun

5 Complete the chart.

Country	Language	Country	Language
England	*English*	China	_____
Spain	_____	Saudi Arabia	_____
Germany	_____	Japan	_____
France	_____	_____	_____
Portugal	_____	(your country)	

Now talk about yourself like this:

I can speak *Spanish*, and I can speak a little English.

For a list of countries and languages, see page 116.

6 What can your classmate do?

A: Can you play a musical instrument?
B: Yes, I can play the *guitar* (but not very well).
   OR No, I can't.

DEVELOP YOUR VOCABULARY

piano   violin

drums   . . .

Now ask about other things.

A: Can you *sew*?
B: Yes, I can. OR No, I can't.

DEVELOP YOUR VOCABULARY

type   cook

paint   . . .

— Life Skills

Telephone numbers • Addresses

1 Review and Build

Review numbers zero to nine. Read these telephone numbers.

1. (213) 924−3076
   area code two one three, nine two four,
   three oh seven six
2. (212) 595−9118
3. 580−2721
4. (214) 617−9999

5. (713) 321−6060
6. (415) 245−2044
7. 889−2171
8. 819−6332
9. (305) 222−2900
10. 741−2469

2 Ask a classmate for his or her telephone number.

A: What's your telephone number?
B: It's *924−3076*.
A: Thanks.

OR

A: What's your telephone number?
B: I don't have a phone.
A: OK, thanks anyway.

3 Read the emergency telephone numbers. Then write *your* emergency telephone numbers.

EMERGENCY NUMBERS	
Police	*9//*
Fire	*9//*
Ambulance	*9//*

Other Emergency Numbers
Dr. Williamson 827−7092
St. Mary's Hospital 349−9400
Mom + Dad (713) 829−1110

EMERGENCY NUMBERS	
Police	....
Fire	....
Ambulance	....

Other Emergency Numbers

Doctor	....
Hospital	....
Parents/friend	....

4 Listen to the conversations and write the telephone numbers.

1. 9 2 9 − 2 9 0 6
2. 3 5 4 − 6 8 7 9
3. 0 4 9 − 1 2 3 5
4. 4 0 9 − 3 0 0 0

Now pretend you are talking on the telephone. Practice the conversation.

5   Review and Build

Review numbers 0 to 1,000. Read these addresses.

1. 60 Regent Street
2. 600 Grand Avenue
3. 6000 Main Street
4. 604 Washington Street
5. 614 Hollywood Boulevard
6. 6040 South Broadway
7. 6640 Main Street
8. 1235 South Broadway
9. 300 Regent Street
10. 102 Washington Street

> **Note:**
> Say address numbers like the time.
>
> | Time | Addresses |
> |------|-----------|
> | 6:04 | 604 Washington Street |
> | 12:35 | 1235 South Broadway |
>
> **Exceptions**
> 60 Regent Street (sixty)
> 600 Grand Avenue (six hundred)
> 6000 Main Street (six thousand)

For Your Information

Zip codes and abbreviations

Look at the envelope.
What's Marty's zip code? What's Beth's zip code? What's yours?

Marty Cruz
12 Regent St.
Los Angeles, CA 90034

Ms. Beth Kramer
330 W. 22nd St.
New York, NY 10011

Look at the abbreviations.

St.   = Street
Ave. = Avenue
Rd.   = Road
Blvd. = Boulevard
Dr.   = Drive
N.   = North
S.   = South
E.   = East
W.   = West

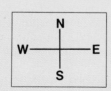

Now write these abbreviations:

Street	_St._
West	_____
California	_____
New York	_____
_____	_____
(your state)	

For a list of states and their abbreviations, see page 114.

Now address an envelope to a friend.

> **Note:**
>
> Put a period (.) after street abbreviations.
> Put a comma (,) between the city and the state.

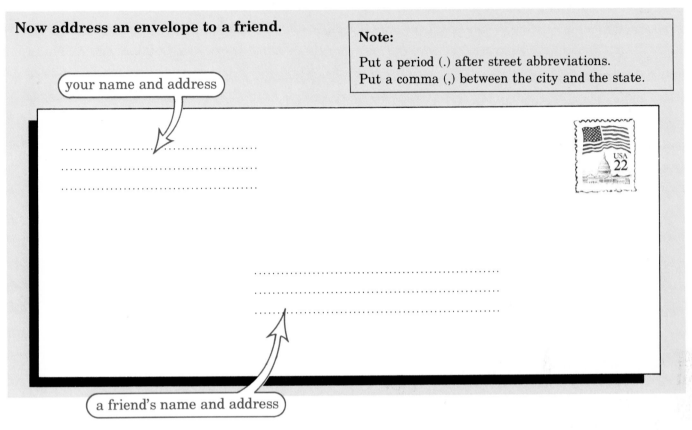

your name and address

a friend's name and address

6 Ask a classmate for his or her address and write it.

A: What's your address?
B: It's *12 Regent Street, Los Angeles, California.*
A: Zip code?
B: *90034.*

7 Listen to each conversation. Then choose the correct address.

1. a. ___✓___   15 Regent St.
   b. _____   50 Regent St.

2. a. _____   14 Grand Ave.
   b. _____   40 Grand Ave.

3. a. _____   1660 Hollywood Blvd.
   b. _____   1616 Hollywood Blvd.

4. a. _____   1303 S. Broadway
   b. _____   3003 S. Broadway

ON YOUR OWN
Do one of the following:

1 **Roleplay:** Turn to the conversation on page 26. You are saying goodbye to a friend and asking for his or her telephone number. Practice the conversation.

2 **Improvise:** Work with two classmates. Change the conversation on page 26. Add your own information. Then present your conversation to the class.

DEVELOP YOUR VOCABULARY

Ways to say goodbye

Bye-bye.   (I'll) See you later.
(I'll) See you soon.   . . .

For pronunciation exercises for Unit 4, see page 110.

REVIEW 2

1 Complete these conversations.

1. A: What 's___ your name?
       ₁
   B: My name _____ Ellen Quon.
              ₂
   A: _____ you from Korea?
      ₃
   B: No, _____ not. _____ from
          ₄   ₅
   Hong Kong.

2. A: Excuse me, _____ you Chris?
                  ₆
   B: No, _____ not. I'm Chris's
          ₇
   sister, Marty.

   A: Oh, you look like your sister.

3. A: What time _____ it?
                 ₈
   B: _____ 3:00.
      ₉
   A: _____ we late?
      ₁₀
   B: No, we _____ .
             ₁₁

4. A: _____ this bus going to Los Angeles?
      ₁₂
   B: No, it _____ . It's _____ to Chicago.
             ₁₃   ₁₄

5. A: Can you roller skate?
   B: No, I _____ , but I _____ ice skate.
           ₁₅   ₁₆

2 Look at the box and the example. Then make four more sentences about Ron.

√play the guitar	√speak English	ice skate
play the violin	speak Chinese	√swim

Ron can play the guitar, but he can't play the violin.
Ron can't play the violin, but he can play the guitar.

Now make sentences about yourself. Use the words in the box.

3 Use _a_ or _an_ before each word.

1. _an_ airport
2. _____ wallet
3. _____ English newspaper
4. _____ violin
5. _____ good hotel

6. _____ guitar
7. _____ umbrella
8. _____ orange sweater
9. _____ early bus
10. _____ friend's name

4 Complete each sentence with the correct word.

1. ___This___ gift is for you.
   This/These
2. We're taking _____ bags on the plane.
                  that/those
3. Whose keys are _____ ?
                   this/these
4. I'm going on _____ bus.
                that/those

5 Lost and Found

Look at this list. It shows what people are bringing with them on the bus.

Marty	Ron	Chris
jacket	keys	sweater
two bags	guitar	bag
umbrella	magazine	keys

34

Now look back at the box on p. 34 and complete these sentences. Use *this,* *these, whose, mine, yours* or the people's names.

1. A: Whose jacket is _*this*_ ?
      1
    B: That's *Marty's* jacket.
             2

2. A: Ron, is that magazine _____ ?
                               3
    B: Yes, it is. Thank you.

3. A: Chris, are _____ your keys?
                    4
    B: No, they aren't. _____ are here.
                         5

4. A: Marty, are _____ your bags?
                   6
    B: Yes, they are.

5. A: _____ guitar is that?
         7
    B: It's _____ guitar.
             8

6 Complete this conversation. Use the correct form of the verbs.

A: What _*are*_ you _*doing*_ next weekend?
                     1. do

B: I _____ home. What _____ you _____ ?
     2. stay   3. do

A: I _____ next Saturday, but on Sunday my husband and I _____ to
     4. work   5. go
   a movie.

7 Match the numbers in column A with the words in column B.

	A		**B**
1.	_e_ 1,000	a.	two hundred and thirty
2.	____ (213)	b.	five fifteen
3.	____ 230	c.	ten thousand
4.	____ 5:15	d.	two one three
5.	____ 5:45	e.	one thousand
6.	____ 10,000	f.	five forty-five

8 Match the sentences in column A with the responses in column B.

	A		**B**
1.	_d_ What time is it, please?	a.	Oh, it's mine.
2.	____ Are you going back to San Francisco today?	b.	We're hungry too.
3.	____ I'm hungry.	c.	No, but I can play the guitar.
4.	____ Whose bag is this?	d.	It's a quarter to six.
5.	____ Can you play the piano?	e.	Yes, we're leaving tonight.

Just for Fun

9 Unscramble the letters. Then match the words in column A with the words in column B.

	A			**B**	
1.	_c_ pyahp	*happy*	a.	yttishr	_____
2.	____ emin	_____	b.	eatl	_____
3.	____ alery	_____	c.	das	*sad*
4.	____ oggin	_____	d.	rousy	_____
5.	____ rayatuSd	_____	e.	nimcog	_____
6.	____ ghurny	_____	f.	nudSay	_____

UNIT 5 Can I Help You?

1 Ron is talking to the desk clerk at his hotel. Listen to their conversation.

1

CLERK: Can I help you?
RON: Yes. How much is a room?
CLERK: $32.00. In advance.
RON: OK.

2

CLERK: Here. Fill out this card, please.
RON: Can I borrow a pen, please?
CLERK: Sure. Here.
RON: Thanks. . . . Excuse me, what's the date today?
CLERK: It's the 14th.

3

CLERK: Say, what kind of work do you do? Are you a musician?
RON: Huh? Oh, no. I'm an actor. But I don't have a job right now.
CLERK: Oh.

4

CLERK: Here's your key. You're in room 304. It's on the third floor.
RON: Where's the elevator?
CLERK: It's over there. On your right.
RON: Thanks.

2 Answer the questions. Begin your answers with _It's_ . . .

1. How much is a room?
2. Whose pen is it?
3. What's the date?
4. Where's the elevator?

3 Warm Up

Borrow something from someone.

A: Can I borrow _a pen_, please?
B: Sure. Here.
A: Thanks.

Now return it.

A: Here's your _pen_. Thank you.
B: You're welcome.

Practice

A.

1 Review and Build

Complete these sentences with *a* or *an*.

1. Marty Cruz is __*a*__ secretary.
2. Marty's father is ____ restaurant manager, and her mother is ____ housewife.
3. Her brother Ricardo is ____ electrician, and his wife is ____ nurse.
4. Her sister Ana is ____ actress.

5. Her sister Chris is ____ police officer, and Chris's husband is ____ teacher.
6. Marty's ex-husband, George, is ____ telephone operator. He's also ____ football coach.

2 Ask what your classmates do.

A: What kind of work do you do?
B: I . . . What do you do?
A: I . . .

For other kinds of occupations, see p. 115.

> ## DEVELOP YOUR VOCABULARY
>
> I'm a factory worker.
> I work in a hotel.
> I don't have a job right now.
> . . .

PROFESSION

secretary

restaurant manager

housewife *or* homemaker

electrician

nurse

actress

police officer

teacher

telephone operator

football coach

3 Study the spelling.

add -s to most nouns	add -es after s and ch	after a consonant change y to i and add -es	change f to v and add -s
electrician electricians	actress actresses coach coaches	secretary secretaries	housewife house**wives**

4 Write the plural of these words.

Singular	Plural
an accountant	*accountants*
a waitress	_____
a wife	_____
an employee	_____
a class	_____
an English class	_____
a family	_____

5 Note these exceptions.

Singular	Plural
a child	children
a man	men
a woman	women

6 Ask questions about the people at Beth Kramer's hotel.

Who's that?	That's Julie Washington.

A: Who's that?
B: That's *Julie Washington.*
A: Is *she* an employee at the hotel?
B: *Yes, she is. She's a receptionist.*

A: And who are they?
B: They're *Mr. and Mrs. Alvarez.*
A: Are they employees at the hotel?
B: *No,* they *aren't.* They're *guests.*

Julie Washington and Bob Vespi/receptionists

Mr. and Mrs. Alvarez/guests

Beth Kramer/guest

Vonda Lupe and Helen Tate/waitresses

Jane Wu and Eric White/accountants

Matthew Barnes and Jeffrey Madison/guests

7 Write three sentences like these about the people in the picture in Exercise 6.

Julie Washington is a receptionist at the Plaza Hotel.
Mr. and Mrs. Alvarez are guests there.
Beth Kramer is a guest there.

B.

1 Find the places in the picture and say each sentence.

The elevator is	**near**	the stairs.
The soda machine is	**next to**	the manager's office.
The manager's office is	**across from**	the elevator.
The drinking fountain is	**between**	the elevator and the stairs.
The manager's office is	**on the left.**	
The elevator is	**on the right.**	
The telephones are	**in the corner.**	
Room 202 is	**upstairs.**	
Room 304 is	**on the third floor.**	
The restrooms are	**down the hall.**	

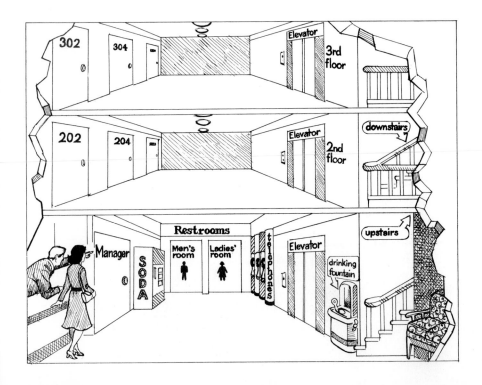

Note: Say room numbers like the time and addresses.

Time	**Address**
3:04	304 Main St.
11:45	1145 Broadway

Room	**Exceptions**
room 304	room 100
room 1145	room 1000

2 Pretend you are the desk clerk at Ron's hotel. A classmate is a guest. Look at the picture on page 39 and tell the guest where things are.

GUEST: Excuse me. Where's *the ladies' room?*
CLERK: It's *down the hall.*
GUEST: And where are *the telephones?*
CLERK: They're *in the corner.*

> **Note:** Plural possessive
> **regular**: ladies' room
> **irregular**: men's room

3 Ask where things are in your school.

A: Excuse me. Where's the *director's office?*
B: It's *room 311.* It's *on the third floor.*

A: Excuse me. What room is *Ms. Barrett* in?
B: *She's* in *room 419.*

DEVELOP YOUR VOCABULARY

library
teachers' room
. . .

4 Pretend you are waiting for a classmate. Write a note and tell him or her where you are.

> Carla —
> I'm making a
> phone call. The
> telephones are down
> the hall near the
> ladies' room. I'll
> meet you there.
>
> Ana

5 Dictation

Ron is talking to another guest at his hotel. Listen to their conversation. Then listen again and complete it.

RON: _____ ?
 1
MAN: It's across from the elevators, on the left.
RON: _____ ?
 2
MAN: Where are you from?
RON: _____ ?
 3
MAN: Denver.
RON: _____ ?
 4
MAN: I'm a teacher. What kind of work do you do?
RON: _____ .
 5
MAN: Well, you're in the right town for that.

Now pretend you're looking for something at your school. Practice the conversation with a classmate.

Just for Fun

6 Continue the conversation in Exercise 5.
Look at the picture and ask for
prices and change.

A: How much is a *soda?*
B: *75¢.*
A: Do you have change for a *dollar?*
B: Yes, I think so.   OR   No, sorry, I don't.

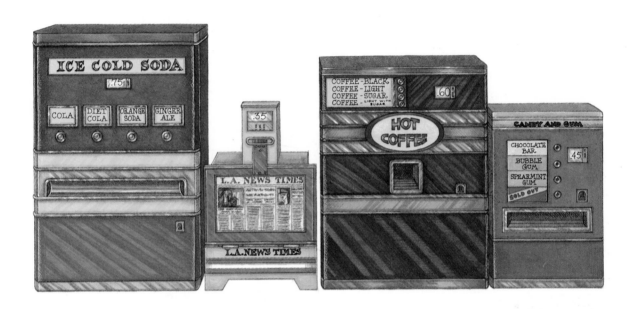

For Your Information

Dollars and cents

penny   nickel   dime   quarter   a dollar   five dollars

Say these prices.

.50	75¢	$1.00	$2.00
fifty cents		a dollar OR one dollar	

Say these prices two ways.

$1.50	$2.50	$2.95	$3.95

one fifty
OR one dollar and fifty cents

Life Skills

Ordinal numbers • Dates

1 Say the ordinal numbers.

1st first	11th eleventh	40th fortieth
2nd second	12th twelfth	50th fiftieth
3rd third	13th thirteenth	60th sixtieth
4th fourth	----------------------	70th seventieth
5th fifth	20th twentieth	80th eightieth
6th sixth	21st twenty-first	90th ninetieth
7th seventh	----------------------	100th one hundredth
8th eighth	30th thirtieth	OR a hundredth
9th ninth	31st thirty-first	
10th tenth	----------------------	

2 Say the months of the year. Then ask and answer questions like this:

A: What's the *first* month of the year?
B: *January.*
A: What's the *last* month of the year?
B: *December.*

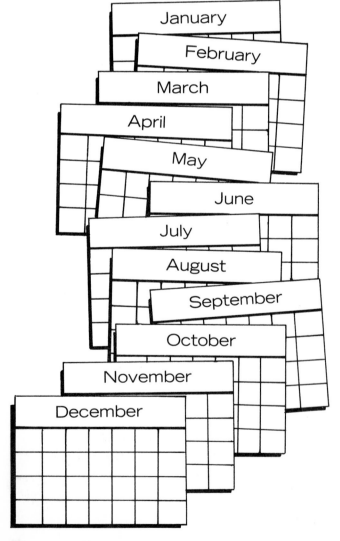

January
February
March
April
May
June
July
August
September
October
November
December

3 Read these dates.

1. First Airplane Flight
December 17, 1903
(December seventeenth, nineteen-oh-three)

2. First Man on the Moon
July 20, 1969

3. Dedication of the Statue of Liberty
October 28, 1886

4. First President of the United States, George Washington
February 4, 1789

5. First Telephone Call from New York to San Francisco
January 25, 1915

4 Find out the date.

A: What's the date (today)?

B: It's *September 14.*

5 Ask and answer the question:

A: When's your birthday?

B: It's . . .

For Your Information

Writing the date

Write the date like this: September 14, 1988

Abbreviations

Jan.	Aug.
Feb.	Sept.
Mar.	Oct.
Apr.	Nov.
-----	Dec.

Note:

Do not abbreviate
May, June and July.

Now write the date like this:

Sept. 14, 1988   OR   9/14/88

                       month day year

Write today's date three ways.

1. _____   2. _____   3. _____

6 Listen to the conversations. Then write the dates.

1. *February 13* _____   3. _____
2. _____   4. _____

7 This is a registration card from Ron's hotel. Fill it out for yourself.

OASIS HOTEL
266 Washington Blvd.
Los Angeles, CA 90018
(213) 424-5000

OASIS HOTEL

ROOM NO. *212*
RATE *$ 32.00*

NAME_____

Last Name   First Name   Middle Initial

ADDRESS_____

Number   Street   Apartment

_____

City   State   Zip Code

CAR MAKE AND MODEL_____

GUEST'S SIGNATURE_____

DATE_____

TELEPHONE_____

OCCUPATION_____

LICENSE NO._____

ON YOUR OWN

Do one of the following:

1 Roleplay: Turn to the conversation on page 36. Pretend you are checking into a hotel or motel. Practice the conversation.

2 Improvise: Work with one classmate. Change the conversation on page 36. Add your own information. Then present your conversation to the class.

For pronunciation exercises for Unit 5, see page 110.

UNIT 6 How Was Your Vacation?

1 Marty was on vacation last week. Today is her first day back at work. Listen to the conversation.

1

HELEN: Hey, Marty. How was your vacation?
MARTY: Hi, Helen. Oh, it was great, thanks. The weather was beautiful.

2

HELEN: Are you doing anything after work today?
MARTY: Uh-uh.
HELEN: Good. Let's go get a cup of coffee, and you can tell me all about Phoenix.
MARTY: OK.

3

CLERK: Can I help you?
HELEN: I'd like a cup of coffee, please.
MARTY: The same for me.
CLERK: Milk and sugar?
HELEN: No sugar.
MARTY: Just black for me.

4

HELEN: My treat.
MARTY: Oh, thanks.
HELEN: How much is it?
CLERK: One-twenty. . . . Thank you. Have a nice evening.
HELEN: You too.

2 Say *That's right* or *That's wrong.*

1. Marty was on vacation last week.
2. The weather was not nice in Phoenix.
3. Helen and Marty are having coffee.
4. A cup of coffee is $1.20.

3 Warm Up

Get a friend's attention and ask about the weekend or the day.

A: Hey, *Jiro*, how was your weekend?
   OR How was your day?
B: It was *great*, thanks. How was yours?
A: It was . . .

DEVELOP YOUR VOCABULARY

wonderful	terrific
pretty good	. . .

44

Practice

A.

Where	were	you	yesterday? last week?	I	was	on vacation. home.
	was	he she	last month? last year?	He She	wasn't	
	were	they		They	were weren't	

How	was	the weather?	It	was	very nice.
				wasn't	

was not = wasn't
were not = weren't

1 Read about Chris, Jim and Marty.
Complete the paragraphs with the correct words.

Chris and Jim are from San Francisco.
They ___weren't___ in San Francisco last
<small>1. wasn't/weren't</small>
week. They _____ in Phoenix. They
<small>2. was/were</small>
_____ on vacation.
<small>3. was/were</small>
Marty is from Los Angeles, but she
_____ at home last week. She
<small>4. wasn't/weren't</small>
_____ on vacation with Chris and
<small>5. was/were</small>
Jim. They _____ all at Chris and Marty's
<small>6. was/were</small>
grandparents' house in Phoenix.

Note: Plural possessive
grandparents' house

2 Where were these people last week?

1. A: Where *were Chris and Jim* last week?
   B: I think *they were* in *Phoenix*.

1. Chris and Jim

2. Marty

3. Beth

4. Richard and Ellen Quon

5. Mr. and Mrs. García

6. Jeff

3 Review and Build

Look at the map and find the cities Ron passed through. Then ask and answer questions like this:

A: Where was Ron on September *6?*

B: He was in *Houston.*

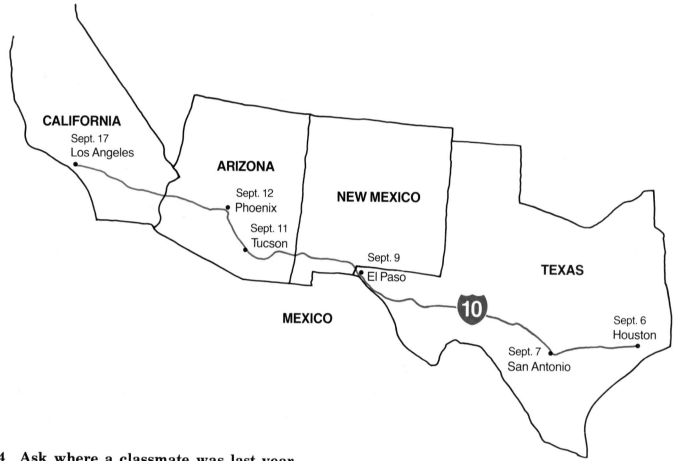

4 Ask where a classmate was last year.

A: Where were you last year at this time?

B: I was *in Colombia.* How about you?

A: I was *here in Los Angeles.*

Now write about a classmate and yourself like this:

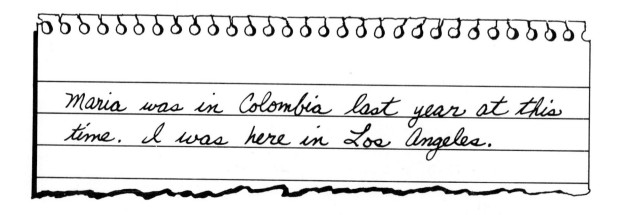

Maria was in Colombia last year at this time. I was here in Los Angeles.

Just for Fun

5 Choose one of these captions for each newspaper photo.

The weather was terrible yesterday.
OR *The weather was beautiful yesterday.*

1

2

3

4

6 Ask about the weather in different places.

A: How's the weather in *New York* right now?
B: It's *cold.*

Now ask about the weather in a classmate's country.

For more words to describe the weather, see page 114.

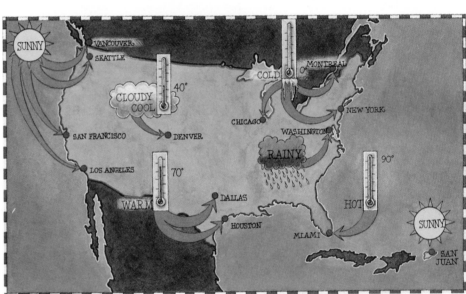

For Your Information

Temperature

Fahrenheit

| 104° | 86° | 68° | 50° | 32° | −4° |

| 40° | 30° | 20° | 10° | 0° | −20° |

Centigrade

In the United States, people use the Fahrenheit system for the temperature. Look at the newspaper weather report and ask questions like this:

A: How was the weather in *Cairo* yesterday?
B: It was *hot.* It was *90* degrees.

THE WEATHER
Yesterday's Temperatures

City	Temp. at noon
Beijing	62
Cairo	90
Hong Kong	83
Madrid	76
Mexico City	68
Moscow	63
New York	49
Ottawa	39
Rome	71
Sydney	65
Tokyo	70
Toronto	42

B.

Were	you they	here last weekend?	Yes,	I	**was.**	No,	I	**wasn't.**
				we they	**were.**		we they	**weren't.**
Was	he she it			he she it	**was.**		he she it	**wasn't.**

1 Where was Jeff last weekend? Listen and complete the paragraph.

Jeff and his grandparents _weren't_ home last
                                    1
weekend. They _____ at a baseball game on
                    2
Saturday, and they _____ at Disneyland on
                         3
Sunday. The baseball game _____ boring,
                               4
but Disneyland _____ fun. The weather
                    5
_____ beautiful, and Jeff and his grandparents
   6
_____ there all day. Sunday night, they
   7
_____ all very tired but happy.
   8

2 Look at Exercise 1 and ask and answer questions.

1. Jeff/at home last weekend
A: Was Jeff at home last weekend?
B: No, he wasn't.
2. Jeff's grandparents/at home last weekend
3. Jeff and his grandparents/at Disneyland on
   Saturday
4. the baseball game/fun
5. Jeff and his grandparents/at the baseball
   game on Saturday
6. Disneyland/fun
7. the weather/terrible
8. Jeff/tired on Sunday night

3 **Marty's friend Helen and Helen's husband, Edward, weren't home last weekend. Find out where they were. Listen and complete the paragraphs.**

Helen _and_ Edward weren't home _____ weekend.
  1   2
_____ were in San Diego _____ Dot and George Eldred.
  3   4
Helen, Edward, Dot and George _____ good friends. _____
                                    5   6
Saturday, they were _____ the San Diego Zoo_____ day.
                         7   8
 On Sunday, they _____ at Sea World. The weather was
                      9
perfect. It _____ sunny and cool.
               10
 Helen _____ Edward's kids _____ with them _____
            11   12   13
San Diego. Tracy _____ at her aunt's house, and Edward Jr.
                      14
was _____ a friend's _____ all weekend.
       15   16

4 **Look at Exercise 3. Pretend you are Helen or Edward and answer questions about your weekend.**

1. you/home last weekend
A: Were you home last weekend?
B: No, I wasn't.
2. Where/you
3. Where/you on Saturday

4. Where/you on Sunday
5. How/the weather
6. your kids/in San Diego with you
7. Where/Tracy
8. Edward Jr./at his aunt's house too

5 **Find out about a classmate's weekend.**

A: Were you home last *Sunday?*
B: No, I wasn't.   OR   Yes, I was.

If the answer is no, continue:

A: Where were you?
B: I was in (at) . . .

6 **Dictation**

Helen is telling her kids about her trip to San Diego. Listen to their conversation. Then listen again and complete it.

TRACY: How was your vacation, Mom?
HELEN: _____ .
                           1
TRACY: Was San Diego nice?
HELEN: _____ .
                           2
TRACY: How was the weather?
HELEN: _____ .
                           3

Now practice the conversation with a classmate. Talk about your last vacation.

Life Skills

Food and restaurants

Just for Fun

a

b

c

d

e

f

1 Match the request with the picture.

1. _b_ I'd like a cup of coffee, please.
2. ___ I'd like a hamburger.
3. ___ A piece of cake, please.

4. ___ Can I have a glass of milk, please?
5. ___ I'd like a chocolate shake.
6. ___ I'd like a donut, please.

2 Look at the menu and answer the questions.

1. What kind of sandwiches can you get?

You can get a ham and cheese sandwich, or . . .

2. What kind of drinks can you get?
3. What kind of milkshakes can you get?
4. What kind of cake can you get?
5. What kind of pie can you get?
6. What else can you get?

3 Review and Build

Your classmate looks at the menu and answers your questions. Ask questions like this:

YOU: How much is *a roast beef sandwich?*
CLERK: *$3.95.*

KING'S FAST FOOD
Menu

Sandwiches	
Roast beef	$3.95
Ham and cheese	2.95
Tuna fish	2.00
Hamburger	2.50
Side orders	
French fries	.75
Coleslaw	.65
Drinks	
Coffee or tea	.60
Milk	.75
Coke, Tab, 7-Up, orange soda	.75
Chocolate, vanilla or strawberry milkshake	1.75
Desserts	
Chocolate cake	1.50
Apple pie	1.00
Donut	.50

50

4 Make a suggestion.

A: I'm *thirsty*. Let's go get *something to drink*.
B: OK.   OR   Sorry, I can't right now.

5 Order a cup of coffee.

YOU: I'd like *a cup of coffee*, please.
CLERK: Milk and sugar?
YOU: Yes, please.   OR   Just milk.
      OR   No, black, please.

DEVELOP YOUR VOCABULARY

a bite to eat	a pizza
something to eat	. . .

Note:
go get = go and get

6 Dictation

Listen to the conversation. Then listen again and write the things Helen and Marty are having for lunch.

CLERK: Can I help you?
HELEN: Yes. Can I have _____?
                              1
MARTY: And I'd like _____.
                              2
CLERK: Anything else?
MARTY: Yes, _____.
                              3
HELEN: Nothing else for me.
CLERK: OK. _____.
                              4
      Coming right up.

Now pretend you and a classmate are in a fast-food restaurant. Look at the menu on page 50 and order something to eat or drink.

7 Practice the conversation in Exercise 6 again. End your conversation like this:

CUSTOMER: How much is it?
CLERK: That's . . ., thank you. Have a nice day.
CUSTOMER: You too.

ON YOUR OWN

Do one of the following:

1 **Roleplay:** Turn to the conversation on page 44. Pretend you and a friend are working at an office. Practice the conversation.

2 **Improvise:** Work with two classmates. Change the conversation on page 44. Add your own information. Then present your conversation to the class.

For pronunciation exercises for Unit 6, see page 111.

```
KING'S FAST FOOD
9/16/88

1 roast beef sandwich    3.95
1 hamburger              2.50
1 coffee                  .60
1 Coke                    .75
1 piece chocolate cake   1.50
                         9.30
              TAX         .72
            TOTAL       10.02

THANK YOU
COME AGAIN
```

REVIEW 3 _____

1 Complete this chart with singular and plural words.

Singular	Plural
an actress	*actresses*
_____	restaurant managers
_____	electricians
a teacher	_____
_____	English teachers
a policewoman	_____
_____	employees
_____	salesmen
a secretary	_____
_____	housewives

2 Write questions with *Who* and complete the answers.

1. A: *Who are they* _____ ?
   B: _____ Matthew Barnes and Jeffrey Madison.

2. A: _____ ?
   B: That _____ Beth Kramer.

3. A: _____ ?
   B: _____ Julie Washington. She's _____ receptionist at the hotel.

4. A: _____ ?
   B: Mr. and Mrs. Alvarez. They _____ guests at the hotel.

5. A: _____ ?
   B: Jane Wu. She _____ _____ accountant.

3 Look at this plan of the third floor of a school.

A	300	302	304	306	
					B
	301	303	305	307	308

Now complete these sentences. Use the words in the box.

1. Room 302 is *next to* room 304.
2. Room 305 is _____ room 303 and room 307.
3. Room 401 is _____ .
4. Room A is _____ room 302.
5. Room 306 is _____ room 307.
6. Room A is _____ .
7. Room 308 is _____ .
8. Room 207 is _____ .

across from	next to
near	on the left
between	downstairs
upstairs	in the corner

4 Match the numbers in column A with the words in column B.

A		B	
1.	*e* 60¢	a.	a nickel
2.	_____ $60.00	b.	twenty-five dollars
3.	_____ 5¢	c.	a dime
4.	_____ 10¢	d.	a dollar
5.	_____ 25¢	e.	sixty cents
6.	_____ $25.00	f.	a quarter
7.	_____ 1¢	g.	sixty dollars
8.	_____ $1.00	h.	a penny

5 Put the months of the year in the correct order.

____ Sept.   ____ June   ____ July   ____ May
____ Mar.   ____ Aug.   ____ Apr.   ____ Dec.
_1_ Jan.   ____ Nov.   ____ Feb.   ____ Oct.

6 Look at this chart and make a sentence about each person.

Name	Birthday
Beth	1/15
Ron	5/12
Marty	11/30
Jim	8/23
Ellen	3/1
_____ (your name)	_____

Beth's birthday is January fifteenth.

7 Complete this conversation with *was, wasn't, were* and *weren't*.

A: Where __were__ you last night? _____
   1   2
   you at home?

B: No, I _____ . My husband and I
         3
   _____ at the movies. How about you?
      4
   _____ you and your husband at home?
      5

A: No, we _____ . I _____ at work, and
          6   7
   my husband _____ at his sister's.
                  8
   How _____ the movie?
         9

B: Oh, it _____ great.
             10

8 Ask questions with these words. Then answer them with your own information.

1. you/at home last night
Were you at home last night?
2. your friend/at school yesterday
3. the weather/nice last weekend

4. you/tired last night
5. Where/you yesterday at 5:00
6. How/the weather yesterday
7. Where/your friends last Sunday

Just for Fun

9 Marty wrote a note in code to her sister Ana. Each number = a letter.

For example: 8 = T   10 = O

Can you read the note? (Remember: The note is from Marty to Ana.)

```
7 6 7—
                 O          T
       5 7 6   4 10 1   11 9 9 8   11 9
T O                T              T
8 10 6 15 14 12 8   6 9 7 3   8 12 9
          T O       T T          O T
9 2 9 13 7 8 10 3   7 8   8 12 9   12 10 8 9 2
                       T
               11 7 3 8 4
```

It Has a Great View

1 A landlord is showing Ron an apartment. Listen to their conversation.

1

RON: How many bedrooms does it have?
MR. GALLO: It has one bedroom.
RON: Does it have a dining room?
MR. GALLO: No, it doesn't. But it has a large living room with a dining area.

2

MR. GALLO: This is the living room.
RON: What a big room! And it has a great view.

3

MR. GALLO: This is the kitchen.
RON: Is that a new refrigerator?
MR. GALLO: No, it isn't. But it's in good condition.

4

RON: And where's the bedroom?
MR. GALLO: The bedroom and the bathroom are down the hall.

2 Say *That's right* or *That's wrong*.

1. Mr. Gallo is the landlord.
2. The apartment has a big living room.
3. The refrigerator is new.
4. The bedroom is down the hall.

3 Warm Up

Give a friend a tour of Ron's apartment.

YOU: This is the *bedroom*.
FRIEND: And where's the *kitchen*?
YOU: It's over here.
  OR It's down the hall.

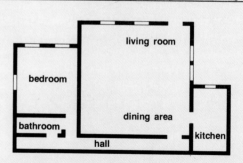

Now draw a picture of your home. Show it to the class.

This is *the living room*. This is *the kitchen*. This is *my bedroom*. And this is *my son's bedroom*.

——Practice——

A.

What a great view! What small rooms!	**Note:** You can use an exclamation point (!) for emphasis.

1   Look at these apartments. Say what you think of them.

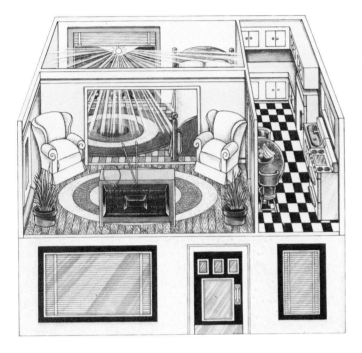
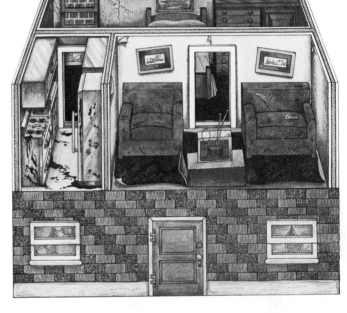

A 1. modern/building
What a modern building!
2. nice/view
3. big/rooms
4. comfortable/chairs
5. clean/kitchen
6. sunny/bedroom

B 1. old/building
What an old building!
2. ugly/view
3. small/rooms
4. uncomfortable/chairs
5. dirty/kitchen
6. dark/bedroom

2   Ron is talking to his mother in Houston. He's telling his mother about the apartment in Mr. Gallo's building. Listen and choose the answers to his mother's questions.

1. landlord	✓ friendly		___ unfriendly	
2. building	___ new		___ old	
3. apartment	___ clean		___ dirty	
4. couch	___ comfortable		___ uncomfortable	
5. neighborhood	___ dangerous		___ safe	
6. neighbors	___ noisy		___ quiet	

55

Just for Fun _____

3 Look at the list of adjectives in Exercise 2. Ask and answer questions like this:

A: What's the opposite of *friendly?*
B: *Unfriendly.*

Now pretend you are Ron's mother or father. Ask Ron the questions in Exercise 2.

1. YOU: How's the landlord? Is he friendly?
   RON: Yes, he is. He's very friendly.
2. YOU: How about the building? Is it new?
   RON: No, it isn't. It's old.

---

4 Ron is describing the rooms in the apartment to his parents. Read these sentences.

> The living room is big, **and** it's sunny.
> OR The living room is big **and** sunny.

> The living room is big, **but** it's dirty.
> OR The living room is big **but** dirty.

Now combine these sentences with the words in parentheses.

1. The bedroom is small. The bedroom is nice. (but)
The bedroom is small, but it's nice. The bedroom is small but nice.
2. The kitchen is dark. The kitchen is dirty. (and)
3. The bathroom is old. The bathroom is in bad condition. (and)
4. The dining area is small. The dining area is OK. (but)
5. The chairs are ugly. The chairs are comfortable. (but)
6. The apartment is old. The apartment is cheap. (but)

B.

I You We They	like want need have	big bedrooms. a nice view.	I You We They	don't	like want need have	big bedrooms. a nice view.
He She (It)	likes wants needs has		He She (It)	doesn't	like want need have	

do not = don't
does not = doesn't

> **Note:** verb + s   Exception
> like —→ likes   have —→ **has**
> want —→ wants

1 The Garcías' house is small but comfortable. Look at the picture and talk about the Garcías' house. Use *have* or *don't have*.

1. small house

The Garcías have a small house.

2. small yard
3. garage
4. basement
5. attic
6. pool
7. porch
8. big garden

2 Ellen Quon is Marty's boss. She has a big house. Talk about her house. Use *has* or *doesn't have*.

Ellen Quon *has a big house.*

3 Write two or three sentences about your house or apartment. Then tell the class about it.

I have a big (small) . . . It has . . . bedroom(s), a . . ., a . . . and a . . . It also has a . . .

My apartment (house) doesn't have a . . . (or a . . .). In my opinion, it's very nice (uncomfortable) . . .

```
╔═══════════════════════════════════╗
║ DEVELOP YOUR VOCABULARY           ║
╠═══════════════════════════════════╣
║          patio                    ║
║          balcony                  ║
║          . . .                    ║
╚═══════════════════════════════════╝
```

4 Read about Marty.

Marty is divorced. She and her son live with her parents. Marty likes her parents very much, but she doesn't like their house. It's very small.

Marty wants a house of her own. She doesn't need a big house. She needs two bedrooms—one for her and one for her son.

Now correct these sentences.

1. Marty is married.

Marty isn't married.   OR   Marty is divorced.

2. She and her son don't live with her mother and father.
3. Marty doesn't like her parents.
4. Marty likes their house.
5. She doesn't want a house of her own.
6. Marty wants an apartment.
7. She needs a big house.
8. She doesn't need a house with two bedrooms.

C.

Do	you they	need want have	a big kitchen? a large yard?	Yes,	I we they	do.	No,	I we they	don't.
Does	he she (it)				he she (it)	does.		he she (it)	doesn't.

1 Complete the chart. Look at exercises B1, B2 and B4 for help.

	Yes	No
1. Do the Garcías live in a big house?	___	✓
2. Do they have a big yard?	___	___
3. Do they have a garden?	___	___
4. Does Ellen Quon live in a big house?	___	___
5. Does she have a big yard?	___	___
6. Does she have a garden?	___	___
7. Does Marty have a house of her own?	___	___
8. Does she want a house?	___	___
9. Does she live with her parents?	___	___

Now ask and answer the questions.

1. A: Do the Garcías live in a big house?
   B: No, they don't.

2 Ask your classmates about where they live.

A: Do you live in a house?
B: No, I don't. I have an apartment.
A: What's it like?
B: It's *pretty nice.* It has *two bedrooms and a small living room.*

OR

A: Do you live in a house?
B: Yes, I do. What about you?
A: I . . .

3 Learn about Ron. Listen and complete the paragraphs.

Ron _wants_ to be an actor, and he
_____ to live in Hollywood. Right now, he
   1
_____ in a hotel. The hotel _____
   2
   3   4
expensive, and he _____ _____ a lot
                      5   6
of money. He _____ to find an apartment.
                7
He _____ a small apartment with one
        8
bedroom. He _____ _____ a big living
            9   10
room, but it _____ important. And he
              11
_____ _____ a big kitchen because he
  12   13
_____ _____ to cook.
  14   15
Ron _____ the apartment in
        16
Mr. Gallo's building. He _____it's perfect.
                          17
It _____ in Hollywood. He _____
    18   19
_____ to buy furniture. And the rent
  20
_____ cheap.
  21

4 Ask and answer questions about Ron.

1. Does Ron want to be an actor?
2. Does he want to live in Hollywood?
3. Does he live in a hotel?
4. Is the hotel expensive?
5. Does . . .

Note:		
He	wants needs likes	a small apartment. one bedroom. Hollywood.
	wants **needs** **likes**	**to live** in Hollywood. **to find** a furnished apartment. **to live** alone.

Life Skills

Housing

Just for Fun

1 Try to match the abbreviations in the boxes with these words.

A.
1. _k_ living room
2. ___ dining room
3. ___ building
4. ___ kitchen
5. ___ shopping
6. ___ apartment
7. ___ month
8. ___ elevator
9. ___ wall-to-wall carpet

10. ___ bedroom
11. ___ bathroom
12. ___ utilities
13. ___ house
14. ___ stove
15. ___ transportation
16. ___ air conditioning
17. ___ security deposit
18. ___ refrigerator

a. bldg	**k.** LR
b. hse	**l.** kit
c. DR	**m.** ba
d. BR	**n.** trans
e. util	**o.** elev
f. shop	**p.** mo
g. sec dep	**q.** ac
h. stv	**r.** w/w cpt
i. refrig	
j. apt	

B.
1. _b_ plus
2. ___ with
3. ___ large
4. ___ and

5. ___ near
6. ___ small
7. ___ unfurnished
8. ___ including
9. ___ furnished

a. &	**f.** unfurn
b. +	**g.** nr
c. sm	**h.** lg
d. furn	**i.** w/
e. incl	

2 What do the abbreviations in Exercise 1 mean?

A: What does *f-u-r-n* stand for?
B: It stands for *furnished*.

For Your Information

Renting houses and apartments

You can rent houses and apartments. Sometimes these are furnished. That means that they have furniture. Sometimes they aren't furnished (they don't have furniture).

Sometimes the utilities are included. That means the gas, electricity and water are part of the rent. Sometimes utilities aren't included, and you pay extra for them.

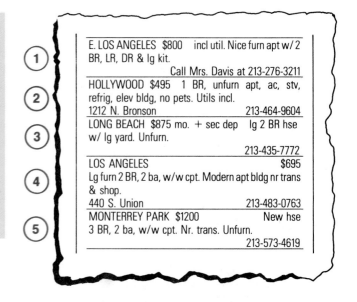

(1) E. LOS ANGELES $800   incl util. Nice furn apt w/ 2 BR, LR, DR & lg kit.
Call Mrs. Davis at 213-276-3211

(2) HOLLYWOOD $495 1 BR, unfurn apt, ac, stv, refrig, elev bldg, no pets. Utils incl.
1212 N. Bronson   213-464-9604

(3) LONG BEACH $875 mo. + sec dep   lg 2 BR hse w/ lg yard. Unfurn.
213-435-7772

(4) LOS ANGELES $695
Lg furn 2 BR, 2 ba, w/w cpt. Modern apt bldg nr trans & shop.
440 S. Union   213-483-0763

(5) MONTERREY PARK $1200   New hse
3 BR, 2 ba, w/w cpt. Nr. trans. Unfurn.
213-573-4619

3 **Look back at the ads for houses and apartments for rent. Ask and answer questions about each ad.**

1. Is it a house or an apartment?
2. Is it furnished?
3. How many *bedrooms* does it have?
4. Does it have a *big living room?*

5. How much is the rent?
6. Are the utilities included?
7. Where is it?
8. What's the telephone number?

4 **Dictation**

Marty's calling about a house for rent. Listen to the conversation. Then listen again and complete it.

MAN: Hello?
MARTY: Yes. I'm calling about the house for rent.
MAN: Yes.
MARTY: _____ ?
　　　　　　　　　1
MAN: Only one.
MARTY: _____ ?
　　　　　　　　　2
MAN: No, it doesn't. But it has a big living room with a dining area.
MARTY: _____ ?
　　　　　　　　　3
MAN: It's $875 a month including utilities.
MARTY: _____ ?
　　　　　　　　　4
MAN: Yes, gas and electricity.

Now practice the conversation with a classmate. Pretend you are calling about one of the ads on page 60.

5 **Read Ron's letter to his sister. Then write a letter to a relative or a friend.**

> September 28, 1988
>
> Dear Barbara,
>
> 　I'm living in Hollywood now. I have a small apartment with a great view. The neighborhood is nice, and my neighbors are very friendly.
> 　My new address is 152 Franklin Avenue, Los Angeles, CA 90027. My telephone number is (213) 350-3817.
>
> 　　　　　Write soon.
>
> 　　　　　*Ron*

ON YOUR OWN
Do one of the following:

1 **Roleplay:** Turn to the conversation on page 54. Pretend you are looking for an apartment and you are talking to a landlord. Practice the conversation.

2 **Improvise:** Work with one classmate. Change the conversation on page 54. Add your own information. Then present your conversation to the class.

For pronunciation exercises for Unit 7, see page 111.

How Do You Like New York?

1 Beth is going to a movie. She's waiting in the ticket line. Listen to the conversation.

1

BETH: Excuse me. Do you have the time?
MAN: Yes, it's a quarter after two.
BETH: Thank you.

2

MAN: It's a beautiful day, isn't it?
BETH: Yes, it is.
MAN: Are you from here?
BETH: Originally. But I live in New York now.

3

MAN: How do you like New York?
BETH: I like it a lot, but I miss California. I miss the weather and the beaches.

4

MAN: Do you have any friends or relatives here?
BETH: My best friend from high school lives here. But my family lives in Chicago now. Uh, you're next.
MAN: Huh? Oh, thanks.

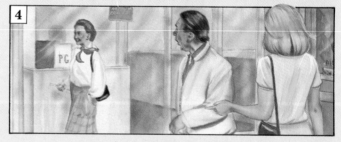

2 Say *That's right, That's wrong* or *It doesn't say.*

1. Beth is wearing a watch.
2. Beth's watch is in her hotel room.
3. The weather isn't nice today.
4. The weather wasn't nice yesterday.
5. Beth is from New York originally.
6. She has relatives in Los Angeles.
7. Beth's best friend is a man.
8. Beth's family lives in Chicago.

3 Warm Up

Find out what time it is.

A: Excuse me, do you have the time?
B: Yes, it's *a quarter after two.*
  OR *It's two fifteen.*
  OR (I'm) Sorry. I don't have a watch.

DEVELOP YOUR VOCABULARY

It's noon.	It's midnight.

Practice

A.

I'm	friendly. The neighbors like	me	
We're		us	
You're		you	
He's		him	a lot.
She's	interesting. I like	her	
It's		it	
They're		them	

1 Learn about Beth. Complete the paragraphs with *me, us, him, her, it* or *them*.

New York is an interesting city. I like

it a lot. I have a lot of friends there.
1

They are wonderful people. I like _____ all
2

very much.

My roommate's name is Alice. She's very

nice, and I like _____ very much. Alice and I
3

are very friendly. We know everybody in our

apartment building, and everybody knows

_____ .
4

My boyfriend's name is Sam. I think Sam is

terrific. I like _____ a lot. I think he likes
5

_____ a lot too.
6

me–

in New York

me and ...

my roommate, Alice

my boyfriend, Sam

2 Review and Build

Find out about your classmates' likes and dislikes.

1. your neighborhood

A: Do you like your neighborhood?
B: Yes, I like it a lot.
   OR   No, I don't like it very much.

2. your house (apartment)
3. your neighbors

4. your job
5. your boss
6. your English class
7. your teacher
8. your classmates
9. your roommate
10. . . .

B.

Where	do	you they	live? work?	I We They	live	on Regent Street.
					work	at Quon, Lunn & Lunn.
	does	he she		He She	lives	on Regent Street.
					works	at Quon, Lunn & Lunn.

1 Look at Beth's address book. Where do the people live?

A: Where *does Marty Cruz* live?
B: *She lives* on *Regent Street.*
A: Oh, where exactly?
B: *She lives* at *12 Regent Street.*

Note:

She lives
on Regent Street.
at 12 Regent Street.

2 Give your exact address.

A: Where do you live?
B: I live at *12 Regent Street.*

3 Review and Build

Look at the chart and ask and answer questions.

1. A: Where does Beth live?
   B: She lives at . . .
2. A: Where does she work?
   B: She works at . . .
3. A: What does she do there?
   B: She's a . . .

Name	Home Address	Place of Employment	Occupation
Beth Kramer	330 W. 22nd St. New York, NY 10023	National Bank	Teller
Sarah Kramer	3617 N. Magnolia Ave. Chicago, IL 60613	Mann's Computer Company	Manager
Mr. and Mrs. Kramer	3617 N. Magnolia Ave. Chicago, IL 60613	St. Luke's Hospital	Doctors

Now ask about Beth's sister and her parents.

4 Interview your classmates. Then make a chart like the one in Exercise 3.

1. A: Where do you live?
   B: . . .
2. A: Where do you work?
   B: . . .   OR   I don't have a job right now. I go to school.
3. A: What do you do there?   OR   What are you studying?
   B: I . . .

5 Beth is telling you about herself. Listen and complete the paragraph.

I live _at_ 330 West _37TH_
         1   2
Street, _IN_ New York City. I _WORK_ at
        3   4
National Bank. _I AM_ a teller _____. My
               5   BANK   6
boyfriend _LIVES_ in New York City too. He
          7
lives _AT_ 66 West Broadway. He works
      8
_AT_ National Business Systems. He's
 9
_A_ computer programmer there.
 10

Now write about yourself and a friend or your spouse.

C.

| It's a nice day, **isn't it?** | Yes, it is. |
| It isn't a very nice day, **is it?** | No, it isn't. |

For Your Information

Conversation openers

Sometimes you want to begin a conversation with someone you don't know very well. You want to be friendly or polite, but you don't know what to say. When this happens, you can open your conversation with a tag question.

a

b

c

d

1 Look at these questions and pictures. Then choose the best question to open each conversation.

1. _C_ It's a beautiful car, isn't it?
2. ___ They aren't very good, are they?
3. ___ It isn't a very nice day, is it?
4. ___ You're new in this office, aren't you?

2 Open a conversation with a classmate.

A: It's a *beautiful* day, isn't it?
B: Yes, it is.

3 Continue the conversation. Ask about your classmate's name and country.

A: Your name's . . ., isn't it?
B: . . .
A: And you're from . . ., aren't you?
B: No, I'm from . . .
  OR Originally. But I live *here* now.

4 Now ask your classmate's opinion of his or her city or town.

A: How do you like *L.A.*?
B: I *really like the people,* and *I love the weather, (but I don't like the traffic).*
OR I don't like it at all.

5 Dictation

Ron is talking to one of his neighbors. Listen to their conversation. Then listen again and complete it.

MING: _____ ?
           1

RON: Yes, I live in apartment 3G.

MING: _____ ?
           2

RON: Hi. I'm Ron.

MING: _____ ?
           3

RON: No. Houston. Why?

MING: You have an accent.

RON: Oh.

MING: _____ ?
           4

RON: I love it. It's a great town.

MING: _____ ?
           5

RON: I'm an actor. How about you?

MING: _____ .
           6

Now practice the conversation with a classmate. Use your own information.

Life Skills

Free time and entertainment

1 **Find out what your classmates do in their free time.**

A: What do you do in your free time?
B: I *read* and *watch TV*.

2 **Find out what kind of movies, TV programs and music your classmates like.**

A: What kind of *movies* do you like?
B: I like *mysteries*.

DEVELOP YOUR VOCABULARY

listen to music   play basketball
go to the movies   . . .

DEVELOP YOUR VOCABULARY

Movies	*TV programs*	*Music*
love stories	movies	rock
science fiction	the news	jazz
comedies	soap operas	popular music
. . .	. . .	. . .

Just for Fun

3 **Can you identify these famous people? (Their names are listed upside down in the box below.)**

Who's your favorite actor? Who's your favorite singer or group?

1

2

3

Stevie Wonder (4)

5

6

7

8

1. Aretha Franklin 2. Whitney Houston 3. Bruce Springsteen 4. Stevie Wonder 5. Julio Iglesias 6. William Shatner 7. Joan Collins 8. The Rolling Stones

4 Look at the brochure. Then ask and answer questions.

1. A: What can you do in Los Angeles?
    B: You can go to . . .

2. A: Where is it?
    B: It's on (at) . . .

3. A: What are the hours?
    B: It's open from . . . to . . . (on . . .)

4. A: How much does it cost?
    B: It's . . . (for adults).

A GUIDE TO LOS ANGELES
Things to see and do . . .

MANN'S CHINESE THEATRE
6925 Hollywood Blvd.
(213) 464-8111
Here you can see the signatures, handprints and footprints of the stars—Elizabeth Taylor, Paul Newman, Clint Eastwood, Frank Sinatra, Donald Duck and many others. Call for movies and show times.

UNIVERSAL CITY STUDIOS
Lankershim Blvd. exit on the Hollywood Freeway
(818) 508-9600
This famous movie studio has three million visitors a year. Movies from this studio include *Jaws, E.T.* and *Conan The Barbarian*. The tour is 2½ hours every day from 10 A.M. to 3:30 P.M. (9 A.M. to 5 P.M. in summer). Adults pay $13.95. Children ages 3–11 $9.95 (under 3 free).

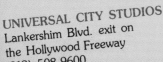

LOS ANGELES MEMORIAL COLISEUM (OLYMPIC STADIUM)
3911 S. Figueroa St.
(213) 747-7111
Home of the 1984 Summer Olympics. Admission $1.50. Children under 12 free.

PUEBLO DE LOS ANGELES
(Olvera Street)
Visitor Information Center at 130 Paseo del Plaza
(213) 239-0200
Two hundred-year-old birthplace of the city of Los Angeles. Old buildings, Mexican shops, restaurants. Open daily from 10 A.M. to 11 P.M. Admission free. Tours at 10 A.M. and 1 P.M.

NEW CHINATOWN
N. Broadway between Ord and Bernard Streets
(213) 461-3665 for information
About 15,000 people live in Chinatown now. It's the cultural center for 150,000 Chinese-Americans in the Los Angeles area. Ethnic shops and restaurants.

Visit Los Angeles

5 Beth wants to see *The Color Purple*. Listen to the recording and choose the correct answers.

1. *The Color Purple* is:
   a. a movie   b. a color   c. It doesn't say.

2. At the time of Beth's call, the theater is:
   a. open   b. closed   c. It doesn't say.

3. Admission for adults is:
   a. $3.00   b. $6.00   c. It doesn't say.

4. Now write the times you can see the movie.
   Show times for *The Color Purple* are

   _____, _____, _____ and _____ .

6 Discuss entertainment in your city.

What can you do in your town for entertainment?
Where is it?
What are the hours?
How much does it cost?

7 Pretend you are on vacation. Write a postcard to a friend or relative. Look at the postcard from Beth to Sam for an example.

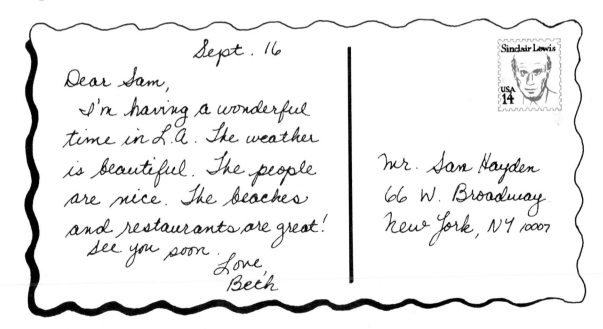

On Your Own
Do one of the following:

1 **Roleplay:** Turn to the conversation on page 62. Pretend you are visiting a city and you are talking to a stranger at a movie or in a store. Practice the conversation.

2 **Improvise:** Work with one classmate. Change the conversation on page 62. Add your own information. Then present your conversation to the class.

For pronunciation exercises for Unit 8, see page 111.

REVIEW 4 _____

1   Rewrite these sentences. Begin with *What*.

1. This apartment is beautiful.
What a beautiful apartment!
2. The view is great.
3. These rooms are small.

4. The refrigerator is dirty.
5. These chairs are comfortable.
6. The kitchen is dark.
7. The neighbors are friendly.

2   Complete these sentences with *and* or *but*.

1. The apartment is old *but* comfortable.
2. The kitchen is big _____ clean.
3. The neighborhood is pretty _____ dangerous.
4. The landlord is good _____ unfriendly.

5. The building is very old _____ very clean.
6. The neighbors are friendly _____ noisy.
7. The bathroom is small _____ dark.
8. The view is nice _____ interesting.

Now make two sentences about your apartment.

My apartment is . . . and . . .   My apartment is . . . but . . .

3   Look at the chart. Make sentences about Ron's apartment. Use *have* or *doesn't have*.

√ refrigerator	wall-to-wall carpeting
√ telephone	√ furniture
air conditioning	√ dining area
dining room	balcony

Ron's apartment has a refrigerator.

4   Complete this conversation about Ron's new apartment.

A: ___*Do*___ you ___*like*___ Ron's new apartment?
               1. like
B: Yes, I _____ .
         2
A: _____ it _____ big rooms?
            3. have
B: No, it _____ . But it _____ a nice view.
        4   5. have
A: _____ Ron _____ to buy new furniture?
             6. need
B: No, he _____ . But he _____ to buy some lamps. The apartment is very dark.
         7   8. want

5   Ask questions about Marty.

1. A: *Does Marty have children* ?
   B: Yes. She has a son.
2. A: _____ ?
   B: No, she doesn't. She lives with her parents.
3. A: _____ ?
   B: Yes, she likes them very much.

4. A: _____ ?
   B: No, she doesn't like it. It's very small.
5. A: _____ ?
   B: No, she doesn't. She only needs two bedrooms.

6 **Complete each sentence with** *me, you, him, her, it, them* **or** *us.*

1. Ron has a new apartment. He likes ___*it*___ a lot.
2. Marty's parents are nice. She likes _____ very much.
3. Alice is Beth's roommate. Beth sees _____ every day.
4. This is Mr. Gallo. Do you know _____ ?
5. These are my friends. Do you know _____ ?
6. My landlord lives in my building. He sees _____ every day.
7. I know _____ ! You're Marty's sister, Chris.
8. We're Mr. and Mrs. García. Do you remember _____ ?
9. Los Angeles is an interesting city, but I don't like _____ very much.

7 **Make questions with the words in column A. Then match the questions with the answers in column B.**

A

1. __*b*__ Where/Beth/live

Where does Beth live?

2. _____ Where/Marty/work
3. _____ Where/Mr. and Mrs. García live
4. _____ What/Beth do
5. _____ What/Beth's parents do

B

a. They live in Los Angeles.
b. She lives in New York.
c. She works in an office.
d. She's a teller.
e. They're doctors.

8 **Complete these questions. Then answer them with your own information.**

1. Your apartment is comfortable, ___*isn't it*___ ?
2. The view is nice, _____ ?
3. You aren't from California, _____ ?
4. Your neighbors are friendly, _____ ?
5. We aren't late, _____ ?
6. It isn't a very nice day, _____ ?

Just for Fun

9 **Read the words in these lists. Choose the one word that is different in each list.**

1. kitchen / bedroom /(stove)/ bathroom / living room
2. ugly / nice / dirty / unfriendly / uncomfortable
3. bldg. / util. / apt. / view / elev.
4. I / he / they / she / us
5. live / want / works / have / miss
6. electrician / teacher / neighbor / teller / nurse

1 Ron is asking his landlord for directions. Listen to their conversation.

1

RON: Hi there, Mr. Gallo. What are you looking for?

MR. GALLO: I can't find my wallet.

RON: What color is it?

MR. GALLO: Brown.

2

RON: There's a wallet behind the seat. Is that it?

MR. GALLO: Pardon?

RON: There's a wallet behind the seat.

MR. GALLO: Oh. That's it. Thanks.

RON: Don't mention it.

3

RON: Say, is there a post office around here? I need some stamps.

MR. GALLO: Yeah. There's one on Hollywood Boulevard next to the movie theater.

RON: Great. Thanks.

4

RON: Oh, I almost forgot. Where can I get some batteries?

MR. GALLO: Why don't you try the drugstore on the corner? Maybe they have some batteries.

RON: Oh, that's a good idea.

2 Correct the statements.

1. Mr. Gallo can't find his car keys.
2. The wallet is black.
3. The post office is on Franklin Avenue.
4. Ron doesn't need batteries and stamps.
5. Mr. Gallo is sure the drugstore has batteries.

3 Warm Up

Look at the ads. Then give the locations of the different stores and services.

A: Where's the *cleaners?*

B: It's on *Hobart Avenue.*

OR It's at *67 Hobart Avenue.*

Michelle's French Bakery
232 Sunset Blvd.

SOAP 'n' SUDS LAUNDROMAT
1555 HOLLYWOOD BLVD.

SPOTLESS CLEANERS
67 HOBART AVENUE

AL'S HARDWARE STORE
5900 SERANO AVENUE

Practice

A.

1 Talk about the neighborhood around your school.

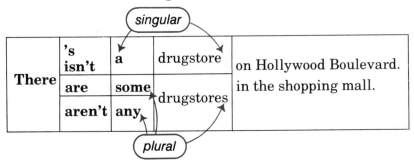

		singular		
There	**'s** **isn't**	**a**	**drugstore**	on Hollywood Boulevard. in the shopping mall.
	are	**some**	**drugstores**	
	aren't	**any**		

plural

> **There is = There's**

Note:

You can be specific:

There are **three** drugstores in the shopping mall.

Or you can be general:

There are **some** drugstores in the shopping mall.

---

2 Look at the ads for the shopping mall near Ron's apartment. What kind of stores and services does it have?

There are some (three) restaurants in the mall.
There's a record store.
There . . .

3 Look at the ads on p. 73 again. What doesn't the shopping mall have?

1. hardware stores

There aren't any hardware stores in the mall.

2. a supermarket
3. bakeries

4. a laundromat
5. a bank
6. . . .

For other kinds of stores and services, see page 115.

4   Learn about Ron's neighborhood. Listen and complete the paragraphs.

There __are__ _____ good stores in Ron's neighborhood.
⎯ 1 ⎯⎯ 2

There' _____ _____ big drugstore. There _____ _____
⎯ 3 ⎯⎯ 4 ⎯⎯⎯⎯ 5 ⎯⎯⎯ 6

supermarkets. And there' _____ _____ small department store.
⎯ 7 ⎯⎯ 8

There' _____ _____ shopping mall near Ron too. There
⎯ 9 ⎯⎯ 10

_____ _____ good shoe stores, and there _____ _____ men's
⎯ 11 ⎯⎯ 12 ⎯⎯⎯ 13 ⎯⎯⎯ 14

clothing stores in the mall. Also, there _____ _____ record
⎯⎯ 15 ⎯⎯⎯ 16

store and a bookstore.

Everything is convenient for Ron. Well, almost

everything. He loves to rent movies, but unfortunately, there

_____ _____ video stores nearby.
⎯ 17 ⎯⎯ 18

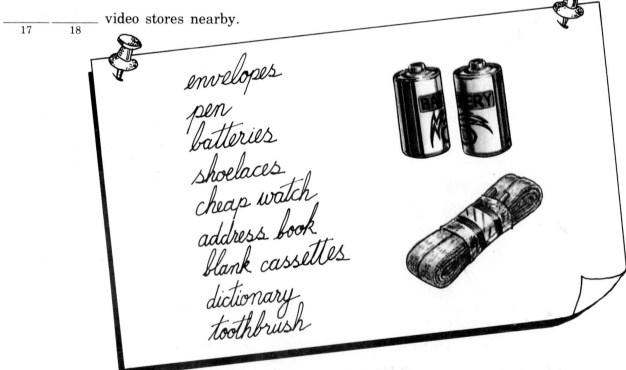

envelopes
pen
batteries
shoelaces
cheap watch
address book
blank cassettes
dictionary
toothbrush

5 Look at Ron's shopping list and answer his questions.

RON: Where can I get _a cheap watch?_
YOU: There's a department store in the mall.
   They probably have _watches._
RON: That's a good idea. Thanks.

OR

RON: Where can I get _some envelopes?_
YOU: Why don't you try the drugstore? Maybe
   they have _envelopes._
RON: That's a good idea. Thanks.

B.

Is there a swimming pool nearby?	Yes,	there is. there are.	No,	there isn't. there aren't.
Are there any movie theaters around here?	Yes, there's one **on the corner of** Venice and Tilden Avenue.			

1 Pretend you are visiting Marty's neighborhood. Ask about different places. Then look at the map and answer.

A: Is there *a swimming pool* around here?
B: Yes, there is.
A: Are there *any cleaners* nearby?
B: No, there aren't.

2 Look at the map and complete the paragraph with *on, between, across from, near, next to* and *on the corner of*.

Marty likes to cook, but she hates to go shopping. Fortunately, she can get everything in the stores *near* her house. There are two supermarkets _____ Venice Boulevard. There's one _____ Tilden and Bentley Avenue. Also, there's one _____ Star's Department Store. There's an excellent bakery _____ the bank. And there's a fruit and vegetable store _____ Girard and Matteson.

Now look at the map again and check your answers.

3 Pretend you're doing errands in Marty's neighborhood. Ask and answer questions.

A: Excuse me. Is there a *post office* around here?

B: Yes, there's one *on the corner of Venice Boulevard and College Avenue.*

A: Thank you.

OR

A: Excuse me. Is there a *post office* around here?

B: No, there isn't.

A: Thanks anyway.

Now ask about places near your school.

4 Beth is doing some errands in Marty's neighborhood. She is asking for help from a police officer. Listen and complete their conversation.

BETH: Excuse me. Where ___can___ I get
     ₁
     something to eat around here?

OFFICER: Why don't _____ try the Westwood
         ₂
         Deli? They have pretty _____
                                   ₃
         sandwiches _____ things.
                    ₄

BETH: _____ the Westwood Deli?
      ₅

OFFICER: It's _____ Venice Boulevard _____
         ₆   ₇
         Westwood _____ Glendon.
                  ₈

BETH: OK. And is _____ a post
                  ₉
      office _____ ?
             ₁₀

OFFICER: It's _____ there— in _____ white
         ₁₁   ₁₂
         building _____ the _____ .
                  ₁₃   ₁₄

BETH: Thanks a lot.

OFFICER: _____ mention _____ .
         ₁₅   ₁₆

Now pretend you are visiting a classmate's neighborhood. Practice the conversation with your classmate. Ask about a place to eat and about another place.

Life Skills

Postal services

1 Review and Build
Read the prices.

(fourteen cents)

(four fifty-six)
OR
(four dollars and fifty-six cents)

 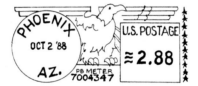 

For Your Information

Postal costs

Letters and postcards usually go airmail (by airplane) in the United States. How much does it cost to send a letter to your country? How much does it cost to send a postcard?

Country	Letter	Postcard	Aerogram
U.S., Canada, Mexico	$0.22*	.14	—
Caribbean islands, Central America, Colombia, Venezuela	.39	.33	.36
All other countries	.44	.28	.36

*prices as of 1987

You can send packages airmail or surface (by truck, train or ship). Airmail is fast, but it's expensive. Surface mail is cheap but slow. The price depends on the weight of the package.

2 You are at the post office. Find out how much it is to send a postcard or letter.

CLERK: Can I help you?
YOU: Yes. How much is it to send *a postcard here in the U.S.?*
CLERK: (It's) *14¢.*
YOU: How much is it to send *a letter to Mexico?*
CLERK: (It's) *22¢.*

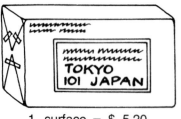

3 Find out how much it is to send a package.

CLERK: Good morning.
YOU: Morning. I'd like to send this package to *Tokyo.*
CLERK: Surface or airmail?
YOU: How much is *surface?*
CLERK: Let's see. It's *$5.20.*
YOU: And how much is *airmail?*
CLERK: It's *$25.70.*
YOU: OK. *Surface.*

> **Note:**
>
> You can say surface or parcel post for addresses in the U.S., Canada and Mexico.

TOKYO 101 JAPAN
1. surface = $ 5.20
   airmail = $25.70

Beijing CHINA
2. surface = $10.40
   airmail = $34.90

CARACAS 1060 VENEZUELA
3. surface = $ 7.80
   airmail = $21.05

Denver, CO 80217
4. surface = $3.57
   airmail = $4.92

MIAMI, FL 31333
5. surface = $3.35
   airmail = $3.51

4 Pretend you are buying some stamps.

CLERK: Can I help you?
YOU: Yes, could I have *ten fourteen-cent stamps*, please?
CLERK: Anything else?
YOU: No, that's it.
CLERK: All right. That'll be *$1.40*, please.

DEVELOP YOUR VOCABULARY

I'd like . . . , please.
Can I have . . . , please?
. . .

5 Dictation

Beth is talking to a clerk at the post office. Listen to their conversation. Then listen again and complete it.

CLERK: _____ ?
          1
BETH: Yes. I'd like to send this package to New York.
CLERK: _____ ?
          2
BETH: Airmail, I guess. How much is it?
CLERK: _____ .
          3

BETH: That's expensive. Oh, well. It's important. OK.
CLERK: _____ ?
          4
BETH: Yes. Could I have five fourteen-cent stamps, please?
CLERK: _____ .
          5

Now practice the conversation with a classmate.

6 Look at Beth's postcard to her roommate, Alice. Add the 19 capital letters and punctuation (2 apostrophes, 7 periods, 5 commas and 1 question mark).

Sept 20 1988

dear alice

how are you doing im having a wonderful time in los angeles its a great town and there are lots of things to do see you soon

love
beth

ms alice fowler
330 w 22 st
new york ny 10011

Now write a postcard to a friend or relative in another city. Use Beth's card as an example.

ON YOUR OWN
Do one of the following:

1 **Roleplay:** Turn to the conversation on page 72. You are looking for the post office or another place. Ask for information and directions. Practice the conversation.

2 **Improvise:** Work with one classmate. Change the conversation on page 72. Add your own information. Then present your conversation to the class.

For pronunciation exercises for Unit 9, see page 112.

Is Marty There, Please?

1 It's Sunday night, and Ron is calling Marty at home. Listen to their conversation.

1

MARTY: Hello?
RON: Hello. Is Marty there, please?
MARTY: This is Marty.
RON: Hi. This is Ron. Ron Wolinski.
MARTY: Oh, hi, Ron. How are you doing?
RON: Pretty good. How are you?
MARTY: I'm fine.

2

RON: Did you have a nice weekend?
MARTY: It was OK. I didn't do anything special. I cleaned and did errands. How about you?
RON: I found an apartment on Friday, and I moved in yesterday.
MARTY: Oh, that's great.
RON: Yeah. I'm real happy about it.

3

RON: Say, would you like to go to a movie tomorrow night?
MARTY: Oh, I'm sorry, I can't. I have to register for my classes at LACC.

4

RON: Well, would like to go to the beach next Saturday? You can bring Jeff.
MARTY: Yeah. Sounds good.
RON: Great!

2 Say *That's right, That's wrong* or *It doesn't say.*

1. Ron and Marty are fine.
2. Marty's weekend was awful.
3. Ron has his own apartment now.
4. Marty is busy tonight.
5. Marty is free next Saturday.
6. Jeff is going to the beach next Saturday too.

3 Warm Up

Invite someone to do something and accept an invitation.

A: Would you like to *go to a movie tonight?*
B: Sure. *(That) Sounds good.*

DEVELOP YOUR VOCABULARY

I'd love to.
I'd like to very much.
. . .

Practice

A.

I have to She has to	register for class tonight.	Tomorrow is Sunday.	I don't She doesn't	have to work.

1 Marty has a busy week. Look at her calendar and say what she has to do.

She has to register for classes on Monday.

Sun	Mon	Tues	Wed	Thurs	Fri	Sat
	register for classes	Take mom shopping after work	Take Jeff to dentist 5:30 meet Ana 7:30	buy my books before class (class begins at 5:30!!)	visit aunt monica and uncle oscar	11:00 meet Ron at the beach

2 Invite a classmate to do something. Your classmate will say no and give an excuse.

A: Would you like to *go get a cup of coffee after class?*

B: I'm sorry, I can't. I have to *go home and study.*

   OR   I'm *meeting my fiancé after class.*

DEVELOP YOUR VOCABULARY	
before ⎫ after ⎭	school lunch the movie the game . . .

3 Work with a classmate. Pretend you are talking to Marty. Invite her to do something this week. Look at the changes on her calendar before you answer.

YOU: Would you like to *go to a movie Monday night?*
MARTY: I'm sorry, I can't. I have to *register for classes.*

YOU: Would you like to *go to a movie after work on Tuesday?*
MARTY: I'd love to. I don't have to *take my mother shopping* after all.

Sun	Mon	Tues	Wed	Thurs	Fri	Sat
	register for classes	Take mom shopping after work	Take Jeff to dentist 5:30 meet Ana 7:30	buy my books before class (class begins at 5:30!!)	visit aunt monica and uncle oscar	11:00 meet Ron at the beach

4 Write a note. Invite a classmate to do something. Your classmate will write back and accept or give an excuse.

Maria –
  Would you like to go to a movie tonight? Rocky VI is playing now.
                    Ana

Sorry, but I can't. I have to help Nina with her homework.
                    Maria

5 Ron's neighbor Ming is inviting him to do things. Listen and note the things Ron *can't* do.

1. ✓ go bowling later
2. _____ go out for a pizza
3. _____ go to a soccer game on Saturday
4. _____ go to a soccer game on Sunday

B.

1 Look at the box. Then find past tense statements in the conversation on page 80.

I You He She We They	moved. cleaned the house. **went** to a movie. **did** errands.

I You He She We They	**didn't**	**move.** **clean** the house. **go** to a movie. **do** errands.

did not = didn't

Note: Add *-d* or *-ed* to regular verbs.
move ⟶ moved   clean ⟶ cleaned

Just for Fun

2 Match the verb on the left with its past tense form on the right.

Base Form

1. __d__ find
2. _____ clean
3. _____ have
4. _____ do
5. _____ stay
6. _____ go
7. _____ play
8. _____ work
9. _____ look for
10. _____ watch

Past Tense Form

a. did
b. played
c. watched
d. found
e. looked for
f. went
g. had
h. worked
i. cleaned
j. stayed

Now complete the chart.

Verb Chart	
Regular Verbs	**Irregular Verbs**
1. clean (cleaned)	1. find (found)
2.	2.
3.	3.
4.	4.
5.	
6.	

See page 113 for more irregular verbs.

3   Say what Ron, Marty and Jeff did last week.

1. Ron/look for an apartment last week/find one on Friday

Ron looked for an apartment last week, and he found one on Friday.

2. he/move into his apartment on Saturday/not do anything on Sunday
3. Marty/work every day last week/stay home every night and watch TV
4. she/go shopping and do errands on Saturday/clean house on Sunday
5. Jeff/go to school every day/have baseball practice after school
6. he/do his homework on Saturday/play with his friends on Sunday

4   Correct the sentences under each picture.

1. Mr. and Mrs. García didn't get up late every day. They got up early.

DEVELOP YOUR VOCABULARY

Irregular Verbs

get up	(got up)
read	(read)
eat	(ate)
take	(took)
. . .	

1. Mr. and Mrs. García got up late every day.

4. Mr. and Mrs. García ate dinner at home Saturday night.

2. They watched TV after breakfast every morning.

5. They went to a movie after dinner on Saturday.

3. Mr. García stayed home every day last week.

6. They took Jeff to Chinatown on Sunday.

5 Review and Build

**Write about what you did last week.
Then tell the class.**

I worked every day, and I had English class on
Tuesday and Thursday nights.

6 Beth Kramer called Marty last weekend. Listen and complete their conversation.

MARTY: Beth! How _are_ you? Where _____
            1   2
you?

BETH: _____ fine. _____ here in L.A. I _____
     3   4   5
here last week.

MARTY: Oh, I _____ wait to see you.
           6

BETH: I _____ in your neighborhood yesterday
     7
morning. I _____ you, but nobody was
          8
home.

MARTY: Oh, I _____ shopping yesterday. And
          9
Mom and Dad _____ at my aunt's.
              10
_____ sorry we _____ you.
   11   12

BETH: That _____ OK. Listen, _____ you
          13   14
_____ anything Wednesday night?
     15

MARTY: I _____ _____ take Jeff to the dentist
        16   17
after work, but then _____ free.
                18

BETH: Good. _____ you _____ _____ meet for
        19   20   21
dinner?

MARTY: Oh, that _____ terrific.
          22

7 Pretend you are talking on the phone to a friend in another city.

A: How was your weekend?
B: It *was OK. I didn't do anything special.*
A: How was the weather?
B: It *rained on Saturday, but it was beautiful
on Sunday.*

C.

Did	you they he she	**buy** a gift for Sam? **visit** Marty?	Yes,	I we they	**did.**
			No,	he she	**didn't.**

1 Beth checked the things she did this weekend. Ask questions about Beth's list.

A: Did Beth *visit Marty?*
B: No, she didn't.

A: Did she *buy gifts for Sam and Alice?*
B: Yes, she did.

> THINGS TO DO THIS WEEKEND
> visit Marty
> ✓ buy gifts for Sam and Alice
> go swimming
> ✓ send a postcard to my mom and dad
> buy a New York newspaper
> take a tour of Universal Studios
> ✓ call the movie theater and find out movie times
> ✓ call Sam

2 Find out what your classmates did last weekend. Ask questions and complete the chart.

A: Did you *go to the beach last weekend?*
B: Yes, I did.   OR   No, I didn't.

Now report the results.

1. *Four* students went to the beach.
2. . . .

WEEKEND ACTIVITIES	
Activity	**Number of Students**
1. go to the beach	4
2. play a sport	_____
3. go to a game	_____
4. watch TV	_____
5. visit friends or relatives	_____
6. entertain friends or relatives at home	_____
7. go out to eat	_____
8. go dancing	_____
9. . . .	_____

3 Dictation

It's Sunday night, and Beth is calling her boyfriend, Sam. Listen to their conversation. Then listen again and complete it.

BETH: Hi, Sam. _____ 1 ?

SAM: Oh, hi, Beth. Yeah, it was all right.

BETH: _____ 2 ?

SAM: No, I didn't. I had the day off.

BETH: _____ 3 ?

SAM: Yeah, I did some errands in the morning, and then I went for a walk. How was your weekend?

BETH: _____ 4 .

SAM: When are you coming home?

BETH: _____ 5 .

SAM: Oh, great! I can't wait to see you.

Life Skills

Telephone calls

1   Make a telephone call. Pretend you are calling Marty. Use your own name and your own information.

MARTY: Hello?
YOU: Hello. Is Marty there, please?
MARTY: This is Marty.
YOU: Hi. This is *Ron.*
MARTY: Hi. How are you doing?
YOU: *Pretty good.* How are you?
MARTY: I'm fine.

2   Now make another call. This time, continue the conversation.

MRS. GARCIA: Hello?
YOU: Hello. Is Marty there, please?
MRS. GARCIA: Just a minute, please.
MARTY: Hello?
YOU: Hi. This is *Ron.*
MARTY: . . .

3   Call someone and leave a message.

A: Hello?
B: Hello. Is *Marty* there, please?
A: I'm sorry, but *she* isn't here right now. Can I take a message?
B: Would you please tell *her Ron* called?
A: Sure. What's your number?
B: *350–3817.*
A: OK. I'll tell *her.*
B: Thank you.
A: Bye.

4   Marty is calling her counselor, Mr. Sedaka, at Los Angeles Community College. Listen and choose the correct answers.

1. Mr. Sedaka is
    a. busy.   (b.) not in his office.
2. The secretary wanted
    a. to help Marty.   b. to take a message.
3. Marty
    a. left a message.   b. asked for information.
4. Registration is from 4:30 to 9:30
    a. in the evening.   b. in the morning.
5. Registration is in the
    a. gym.   b. cafeteria.

For Your Information

Formal and informal language

Americans are often very informal. They use people's first names, they use informal language, and they ask personal questions. They aren't being impolite. They are only trying to be friendly.

Can you choose the informal language in each pair?

1. _____ Hi.
   _____ Good evening.
2. _____ May I speak to Hector, please?
   _____ Is Hector there?

3. _____ Can you tell me where English 100 is?
   _____ Where's English 100?
4. _____ When is it?
   _____ Could you tell me when it is?

Note, however, that sometimes it is a good idea to use more formal language—for example, when you talk to your boss or when you ask a stranger for information.

5 Now, pretend you are calling LACC and asking for information. Ask about the courses on the list.

SECRETARY: Los Angeles Community College. May I help you?
YOU: Yes. Can you tell me where *English 100* is, please?
SECRETARY: Yes, it's in room *109.*
YOU: And could tell me when it is, please?
SECRETARY: Yes, it's on *Mondays, Wednesdays and Fridays from 5:30 to 6:30.*
YOU: Thank you.
SECRETARY: You're welcome.

Los Angeles Community College					
Course	Section	Instructor	Day	Time	Room
Business Math	200	Ms. Smith	MWF	8:00–9:00	330
Business Math	300	Ms. Smith	TTh	7:15–8:45	232
Data Processing	111	Mr. Randall	MWF	5:30–7:00	112
Data Processing	211	Mr. Randall	TTh	7:15–8:45	112
English	100	Mr. Barker	MWF	5:30–6:30	109
English	101	Ms. Wang	TTh	5:30–7:00	204
English	201	Mr. Barker	MWF	6:45–7:45	207
Word Processing	211	Ms. Jaffey	TTh	5:30–7:00	315
Word Processing	212	Mr. Ruiz	TTh	7:15–8:45	313

6 Marty registered for English 201, Word Processing 211 and Business Math 200. Complete her schedule. Then make a class schedule for yourself.

LOS ANGELES COMMUNITY COLLEGE			Class Schedule		
Name _____ Marta García _____		Student I.D. No. __542-04-1484__			
Address _____ 12 Regent St. _____		Tel. __(213) 924-3076__			
City _____ Los Angeles _____		State __CA__		Zip __90034__	
Course	Section	Instructor	Day	Time	Room

ON YOUR OWN

Do one of the following:

1 Roleplay: Turn to the conversation on page 80. Pretend you are calling a new friend. Tell about your weekend and invite your friend to do something. Practice the conversation.

2 Improvise: Work with one classmate. Change the conversation on page 80. Add your own information. Then present your conversation to the class.

For pronunciation exercises for Unit 10, see page 112.

REVIEW 5

1 Look at the box below. Then make sentences like these about Chris's neighborhood:

✓ movie theater	✓ fruit and vegetable store
✓ post office	good bookstore
record stores	✓ banks
✓ supermarkets	swimming pool
Italian bakery	discos

There's a movie theater in Chris's neighborhood.
There aren't any record stores.

2 Complete these questions. Use *is there a(n)* or *are there any*. Then answer them with your own information.

1. _Are there any_ department stores in your neighborhood?
2. _____ post office nearby?
3. _____ children on your street?
4. _____ good bakery around here?
5. _____ hotels around here?
6. _____ shopping malls near your home?
7. _____ video store in your neighborhood?
8. _____ good woman's clothing store in your neighborhood?
9. _____ airport nearby?

3 Match the questions in column A with the answers in column B.

A	B
1. _b_ Is the bakery good?	a. Yes, there is.
2. ____ Where's the post office?	b. Yes, it is.
3. ____ Where are the video stores?	c. It's nearby.
4. ____ Is there a drugstore nearby?	d. They're on Hollywood Boulevard.
5. ____ Are there any discos around here?	e. Yes, they are.
6. ____ Are the restaurants good?	f. Yes, there are.

4 Answer these questions. Use *have to* or *has to* and a verb.

1. A: Would you like to go to the movies tonight?
   B: I can't. I _have to do_ my homework.

2. A: Can Marty come with us?
   B: No, she can't. She _____ at the office.

3. A: Are you free tomorrow?
   B: No, I'm not. I _____ to class.

4. A: Can Ron have dinner with us tomorrow?
   B: No, he can't. He _____ shopping.

5. A: Would you like to get a cup of coffee after class?
   B: Thanks. But I _____ some letters.

6. A: Can Beth go shopping with Marty?
   B: No, she can't. She _____ to the dentist.

5 Complete the chart with the present and past forms of these verbs.

Present	Past		Present	Past
1. stay	*stayed*		6. _____	moved
2. do	_____		7. have	_____
3. _____	worked		8. _____	went
4. _____	found		9. _____	saw
5. watch	_____		10. eat	_____

6 Complete these sentences. Use the past tense of each verb.

Last week Ron ___*found*___ a new apartment. He _____ into it on
              1. find   2. move

Saturday. Then he _____ shopping and _____ a new lamp. He _____
                3. go   4. buy   5. go-*neg.*

to the movies with his new neighbor because he _____ a lot of work.
                                        6. have

Marty _____ also very busy last week. She _____ early every
           7. be   8. get up

day, _____ the house and _____ errands. She also _____ Jeff
      9. clean   10. do   11. take

to the dentist. She _____ anything special on the weekend. Her friend
               12. do-*neg.*

Beth _____ in L.A. She _____ Marty, but she _____ her.
       13. be   14. call   15. visit-*neg.*

7 Ask questions. Begin with *Did*.

1. A: *Did she call her aunt* ?
   B: Yes, she did. She called her aunt yesterday.
2. A: _____ ?
   B: Yes, I did. I went to two department stores.
3. A: _____ ?
   B: No, I didn't. I wasn't hungry.
4. A: _____ ?
   B: No, he didn't. It rained all day.

5. A: _____ ?
   B: No, they didn't. They had the day off.
6. A: _____ ?
   B: Yes, we did. We were home all day.
7. A: _____ ?
   B: Yes, I did. I made a reservation for Monday.
8. A: _____ ?
   B: No, I didn't do anything special.

Just for Fun

8 Look at this box. It has 10 words in the past tense. Can you find the other 8?

W	A	N	T	E	D
E	N	D	Y	O	U
N	H	O	P	N	S
T	A	K	E	E	P
A	D	D	W	A	S
L	I	X	A	N	A
K	D	A	R	K	W
E	A	T	I	A	E
D	O	E	S	T	R
M	A	D	E	Y	E

1 Beth and Marty are meeting at a restaurant. Listen to their conversation.

1

MARTY: Hi. Sorry I'm late.

BETH: Marty, you never change! You're always late!

MARTY: Give me a break! Jeff is sick, and I had to go to the drugstore and get some medicine.

2

BETH: What's the matter with Jeff?

MARTY: He has a cold. He stayed home from school today.

BETH: School? How old is he?

MARTY: Seven. He's in the second grade.

BETH: You're kidding!

3

BETH: So, what's new with you?

MARTY: Well, I'm taking courses at LACC now.

BETH: Oh? Why did you go back to school?

MARTY: Because I have a good future at Q, L & L. But I really need to get my degree first.

4

BETH: Where do you work? Q, L & L?

MARTY: Yeah. Quon, Lunn and Lunn. It's an advertising agency.

BETH: Quon? There was a couple on my flight from New York. Their name was Quon.

MARTY: Not Ellen and Richard?

BETH: That's right. Ellen and Richard.

MARTY: Ellen's my boss. Gee, it's a small world.

2 Say *That's right, That's wrong* or *It doesn't say.*

1. Jeff is sick.
2. Marty took Jeff to the doctor.
3. Marty doesn't have a good future at work.
4. Beth met Marty's boss on her flight from New York.

3 Warm Up

Pretend you are late for a meeting with an old friend. Give an excuse.

A: (I'm) Sorry I'm late. *I had to go to the bank.*

B: That's OK. Don't worry about it.

4 Warm Up

Ask a classmate about his or her family.

A: Do you have any children (brothers or sisters)?

B: Yes, I have *a son and a daughter.*

A: How old are they?

B: *My son's seven, and my daughter's thirteen.*

Practice

A.

Are you	**always** **usually**	late?	You're	usually often	late.
Do you	**often** **sometimes**	drive to work?	You	sometimes **hardly ever** **never**	drive to work.

1 Are you usually late, or are you on time for appointments? Look at the examples. Then talk about yourself.

Marty's *always* late. She's *never* on time for things.
Beth is *sometimes* late, but she's *usually* on time.

What about you?

Note:		
always	=	100% of the time
usually	=	90%
often	=	70–80%
sometimes	=	20–60%
hardly ever	=	10%
never	=	0%

Just for Fun

2 Match the statements with the pictures.

1. _*e*_ She sometimes takes a taxi to work.
2. ____ She always walks to work.
3. ____ She usually takes the subway.
4. ____ He often rides his bike.
5. ____ They always take the bus to work.
6. ____ She usually drives.
7. ____ Sometimes he rides with his daughter.
8. ____ He doesn't have a job.

a

b

c

d

e

f

g

h

Now ask and answer questions like this:

1. A: Does Ellen sometimes take a taxi to work?
   B: Yes, she does.   OR   Yes, sometimes.

3 Now find out how your classmates get to work or school. Also find out how long it takes.

A: How do you get to work (school)?
B: I usually *take the bus*.
A: How long does it take?
B: (It usually takes) About *an hour*.

4 Learn more about Marty. Listen and complete the paragraphs.

Marty has a lot of responsibilities. She works full time. She takes care of her son. And she goes to school at night. She *hardly ever* _____ any free time.
                                                                                    1   2   3

Marty _____ _____ up at 6:30. She makes breakfast for Jeff, and she
             4   5
_____ _____ a pot of coffee for her mother and father. Marty drives to work.
    6   7
She _____ _____ the house at 7:30. But she _____ _____ at 7:15 and
        8   9   10   11
_____ her father a ride to his restaurant.
    12
Marty _____ _____ a day of work. She likes her job, and she _____
            13   14   15
_____ hard. She _____ _____ overtime.
    16   17   18

5 Review and Build

Interview a classmate and take notes.

1. What time do you usually get up?
2. What time do you leave for school (work)?
3. How do you get there?
4. How long does it take?

Now write a paragraph about your classmate. Use your notes. Be sure to indent.

1. 6:30
2. sometimes 8:00
   sometimes 8:30
3. Walk
4. about half an hour

6 Ask your classmates about school or their jobs.

A: How do you like school (your job)?
B: I like it a lot. *It's interesting.*
   OR I don't like it very much. *It's boring.*
A: Do you study (work) hard?
B: *Yes, usually.*
A: Do you stay after school for extra help (work overtime)?
B: *No, hardly ever.*

B.

Why did you **go** back to school?	**(Because)** I want to get my degree.
When did you **begin** school?	I began last year.

1 Find out about these people.

1. Marty Cruz
   - a. A: Where was Marty Cruz born?
     - B: (She was born) In . . .
   - b. A: Where did she grow up?
     - B: (She grew up) . . .
   - c. A: When did she meet her husband?
     - B: She met . . .
   - d. A: Why did she get divorced?
     - B: (Because). . .

I was born in L.A. I grew up here. I met my husband in high school, and we got married after graduation. Unfortunately, we got divorced four years later because we didn't get along. I began night school last year.

2. Mr. and Mrs. García
   - a. Where/grow up?
   - b. What/do in Mexico?
   - c. Why/move to the U.S.?
   - d. When/come here?

We were born in Mexico. We grew up there. I was a cook, and my wife took care of the house and the children. In 1960, I got a good job in L.A., and we moved here. My wife's parents moved to Phoenix in 1975.

3. Ron Wolinski
   - a. Where
   - b. What
   - c. Why
   - d. Why

I grew up in Houston. I was a part-time waiter and a part-time student. I studied acting. I came to L.A. because I want to be an actor. I rented an apartment in Hollywood because a lot of actors live there.

4. Beth Kramer
   - a. . . .
   - b. . . .
   - c. . . .
   - d. . . .

I was born in Los Angeles, and I grew up here. My family moved to New York in 1980. They moved because my grandmother lived in New York, and she was very sick. My family moved to Chicago last year, but I stayed in New York.

2 Dictation

Beth is asking Marty about her boss, Ellen Quon. Listen and write Beth's questions. Then listen again and choose the correct answers.

1. _____

    a. In Hong Kong.   b. In 1942.

2. _____

    a. Their friends live here.
    b. Their relatives live here.

3. _____

    a. Yes.   b. No.

4. _____

    a. In 1969.   b. In 1979.

3 Interview a classmate.

1. Where were you born?
2. Did you grow up there (here)?
3. Did you go to school there (here) too?
4. What kind of work did you do?
5. Why did you (your family) come to the U.S.?

4 Now write a paragraph about yourself. Answer the questions in Exercise 3. Be sure to indent.

_____

_____

_____

_____

_____

_____

Life Skills

Health care

Just for Fun

1 Label the parts of the body.

A. head   forehead
    eye   nose
    ear   mouth
    back   tooth (teeth)
    throat   neck

B. shoulder   chest
    arm   elbow
    stomach   wrist
    hand   finger
    knee   leg
    ankle   toe
    foot (feet)

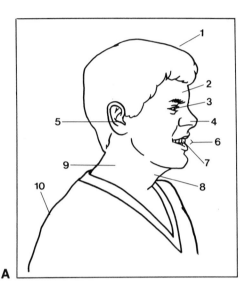

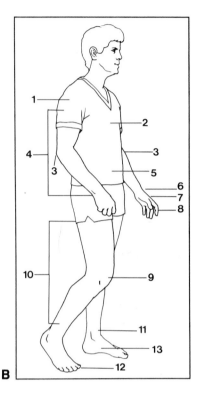

2 What are these people saying? Match the sentences with the pictures.

1. __c__ I have a sore throat.
2. _____ I have a headache.
3. _____ I have a backache.
4. _____ I have a stomachache.
5. _____ I have an earache.
6. _____ I have a toothache.

a

b

c

d

e

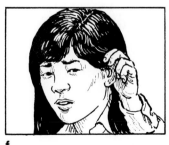

f

Now point to the pictures and ask questions like this:

A: What's the matter with him (her)?
B: He (She) . . .

3 Pretend you're sick.

A: What's the matter?

B: I don't feel good. I *have a headache and a sore throat.*

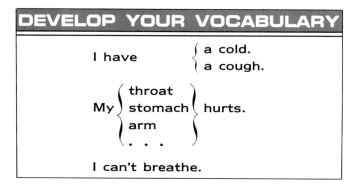

DEVELOP YOUR VOCABULARY

I have { a cold.
{ a cough.

My { throat
{ stomach } hurts.
{ arm
. . .

I can't breathe.

4 Practice the conversation in Exercise 3 again. This time give your partner advice like this:

A: Why don't you *take a couple of aspirins?*

B: That's a good idea.   OR   No, I'm OK.

DEVELOP YOUR VOCABULARY

get some cough medicine
lie down and rest
go see a doctor
. . .

5 Here are some medicines and other things you can find in a drugstore. Look at the pictures and write the name of each item in the right place.

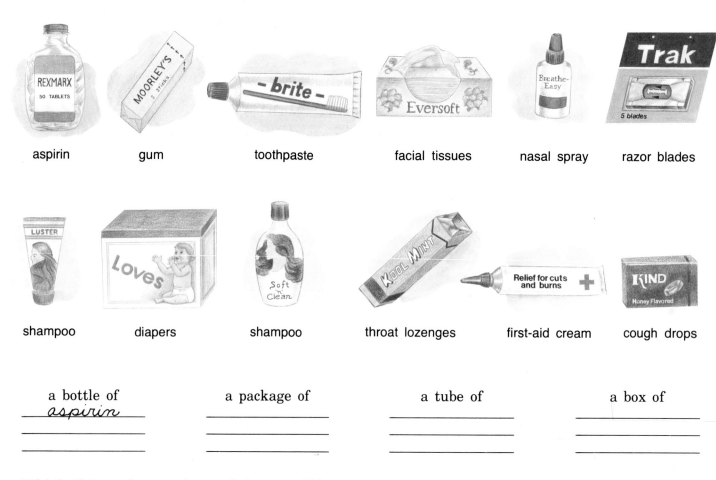

aspirin   gum   toothpaste   facial tissues   nasal spray   razor blades

shampoo   diapers   shampoo   throat lozenges   first-aid cream   cough drops

a bottle of   a package of   a tube of   a box of
aspirin   _____   _____   _____
_____   _____   _____   _____
_____   _____   _____   _____

Which things do people need for a cold?

For Your Information

Making requests

You can be general:

I'd like **some** aspirin.
I'd like **some** toothpaste.
I'd like **some** razor blades.

Or you can be specific:

I'd like **a bottle** of aspirin.
I'd like **one tube** of toothpaste.
I'd like **two packages** of razor blades.

Practice saying what you need. Use the items in Exercise 5.
I need *some aspirin.*   OR   I need *a bottle of aspirin.*

6 Pretend you are sick and can't go to the drugstore. Write a note and ask
   someone to go for you. Look at Mr. García's note to his wife for an example.

> Elena —
>   I'm in bed taking a nap. I don't
> feel very good. Would you get me
> some aspirin and a package of
> throat lozenges? And would you
> buy a box of tissues too, please?
>   Thanks. H.

7 Marty is going to the drugstore. Listen and choose the things Marty is
   getting for her parents.

_____ shampoo
_____ aspirin
_____ throat lozenges
_____ cough medicine
_____ razor blades

_____ cough drops
__✓__ toothpaste
_____ toothbrush
_____ tissues
_____ nasal spray

ON YOUR OWN
Do one of the following:

1 **Roleplay:** Turn to the conversation on page
   90. Pretend you are meeting an old friend.
   Practice the conversation.

2 **Improvise:** Work with one classmate.
   Change the conversation on page 90. Add
   your own information. Then present your
   conversation to the class.

For pronunciation exercises for Unit 11, see page 112.

1 It's Saturday. Ron is meeting Marty at the beach. Listen to their conversation.

1

MARTY: Sorry I'm late. I left on time, but I forgot my wallet. I had to go back and get it. Then I had to stop and get gas.

RON: That's OK. Where's Jeff?

MARTY: Oh, he's playing baseball with his friends.

2

RON: Those are great earrings.

MARTY: Thanks. So what's new? Did you find a job yet?

RON: No, not yet. I went to a couple of agencies, and I answered several ads, but no luck. Actors are a dime a dozen in this town.

3

MARTY: What are you going to do?

RON: I don't know.

MARTY: Are you going to look for something else?

RON: I'm going to have to. I'm almost broke.

4

MARTY: Maybe my dad can help. He manages a restaurant, and he's always looking for waiters.

RON: That would be great! I worked as a waiter in Houston.

2 Answer *That's right* or *That's wrong*.

1. Marty was late because she forgot her wallet.
2. Ron doesn't like Marty's earrings.
3. There are a lot of actors in L.A.
4. Ron needs a job because he doesn't have a lot of money.
5. Ron was a waiter in Mr. García's restaurant.

3 Warm Up

Compliment a classmate.

A: That's *a great tie!*
B: *Thanks.*

A: Those are *beautiful earrings.*
B: *Thank you.*

DEVELOP YOUR VOCABULARY

Thank you.	It's (They're) new. It was (They were) a gift. *My wife* gave it (them) to me. . . .

Practice

A.

1 Look at the box. Then find examples of *going to* in the conversation on page 98.

What	**are** you		do tomorrow?
When	**are** they	**going to**	start their new jobs?
Where	**is** she		look for a job?

I	'**m** '**m not**		
They	'**re** **aren't**	**going to**	go to an employment agency. start Monday. check the newspaper.
She	'**s** **isn't**		

> **Note:** With the verb **go** you can say:
>
> I'm **going to go** to an employment agency.
> OR I'm **going** to an employment agency.

2 **Ron made a list. Then he crossed some things off the list. Say what Ron is going to do and what he isn't going to do.**

He's going to get the newspaper tomorrow morning.
He isn't going to buy a new suit for his interviews.

Ron crossed four things off his list. Why? Can you guess?

TO DO THIS WEEK

Get the newspaper tomorrow morning

~~Buy a new suit for my job interviews~~

Check the ads for part-time jobs tomorrow

Call the Hollywood Talent Agency this week

~~Register for acting classes on Tuesday~~

~~Buy a new toy truck for Jeff~~

Call Mr. García about jobs in his restaurant on Monday

~~Invite Marty out to dinner~~

3 These people are going to change their lives. Read their letters and ask and answer questions about their future plans.

1. Chris and Jim
   a. Where do Chris and Jim live now?
   b. Where are they going to move?
   c. When are they going to move?
   d. Why are they going to move?
   e. What are they going to do there?

Dear Mom, Dad, Marty and Jeff,

   I have some great news. We're going to have a baby. Jim and I are very excited.
   And that's not all. We are going to move to Pleasantville. We bought a house there. We love San Francisco, but we want to live in a small town. We're going to move at the end of the school year.
   Jim is going to teach at the high school in Pleasantville, but I'm not going back to work for a while.

Love,

Chris

2. Mr. and Mrs. García
   a. What/Mr. García do
   b. How old/be
   c. What/buy
   d. Why/go

Dear Chris and Jim,

   Congratulations! Your news about the baby is wonderful. Your father and I are very happy for you.
   Your father and I have some news too. Your father's going to be sixty-two next week, and he's going to retire. We're going to buy a new car and take a trip to Mexico with Grandma and Grandpa. We're going to visit all of our relatives there.
   It's going to be a good year for all of us.

Love,

Mom

4 What's going to happen to Beth and Sam? Listen to Sam's conversation with his dad and complete it.

SAM: Dad, I'm _gomg_ _to_ marry Beth.
              ₁   ₂

DAD: Oh. Well, _are_ _you_ sure?
             ₃   ₄

SAM: Yes, _I'm_ sure. _I_ _bought_ a ring yesterday.
         ₅   ₆   ₇

DAD: Well, _She's_ a wonderful woman, but . . . ah . . . but _do_
             ₈   ₉
you love her?
 ₁₀

SAM: Of course, I do. I _didn't_ love Marilyn, and I didn't _love_ Julie, but I _do_
                      ₁₁   ₁₂   ₁₃
love Beth.

DAD: Oh. And when _are_ _you_ going to ask the big question?
                  ₁₄   ₁₅

SAM: Next Friday. Beth's _gomg_ _to_ come back from L.A. next Friday night.
                          ₁₆   ₁₇
I'm going to _ask_ her at the airport.
             ₁₈

DAD: Well . . . congratulations . . . I guess . . .

5 Dictation

Ron is talking to his neighbor Ming. Ming isn't happy with his job. Listen to their conversation. Then listen again and complete it.

MING: How was your day?

RON: _____ . What did you do?
             ₁

MING: I stayed home and thought about my job at the telephone company.

RON: Oh, yeah? _____?
                    ₂

MING: I'm going to quit.

RON: _____?
             ₃

MING: I don't want to repair telephones all my life. I want to get a job as an electrician.

RON: _____?
             ₄

MING: I don't know. I have to find a job first. How about you? Did you find anything yet?

RON: No. _____ . He manages a restaurant.
             ₅

6 Ask your classmates about their plans for the future.

A: What are you going to do next year (after this course)?

B: . . .

Continue with other questions.

A: Where/when/why/what kind/how are you going to . . . ?

B: . . .

DEVELOP YOUR VOCABULARY

get a job
continue studying
. . .

B.

Are you Are they Is she	going to	take another English class? get married? get a raise?	Yes,	I am. they are. she is.	No,	I'm not. they aren't. she isn't.

1 Marty is going to get a promotion. Look at Ellen Quon's notes and ask and answer questions like this:

A: Is Marty going to *be Ellen's office manager?*
B: Yes, she is.
A: Is she going to *have to type in her new position?*
B: No, she isn't.

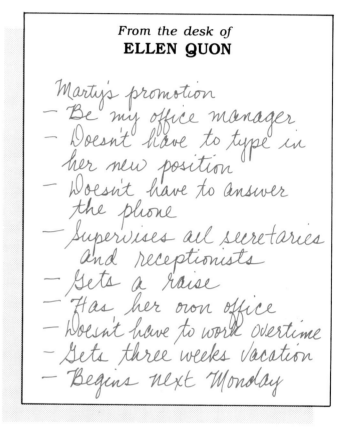

From the desk of
ELLEN QUON

Marty's promotion
— Be my office manager
— Doesn't have to type in her new position
— Doesn't have to answer the phone
— Supervises all secretaries and receptionists
— Gets a raise
— Has her own office
— Doesn't have to work overtime
— Gets three weeks vacation
— Begins next Monday

2 Review and Build

What's going to happen to Marty and Ron? Ask questions and give your opinion.

1. Ron/stay in Los Angeles or move back to Houston

A: Is Ron going to stay in Los Angeles, or is he going to move back to Houston?
B: I (don't) think he's going to . . . (because . . .)

2. Ron/be a successful actor or work in the restaurant business
3. Ron and Marty/fall in love or just become good friends
4. Marty and Ron/get married or stay single
5. Marty/become a vice president of Q, L & L or quit her job and be a housewife

3 Now write the end of the story. Tell what's going to happen to Marty and Ron in your opinion.

— Life Skills —

Employment

Just for Fun

1 Choose the correct word for each abbreviation.

1.	F/T	*full time*	male or female	full time
2.	exper.	Experience	hours per week	experience
3.	vac.	Vacation	part time	necessary
4.	excel.	excelent	words per minute	vacation
5.	yrs.	Years	department	years
6.	min.	minimum	excellent	minimum
7.	nec.	Necessary		
8.	dept.	department		
9.	hrs/wk	hours per week		
10.	P/T	Part time		
11.	wpm	Words per minute		
12.	M/F	Male or female		

---

2 Look at the ads and find a job for these people. Match the ad with the person.

a. _3_ Ron's neighbor Ming wants a job as an electrician.

b. ___ Ming's girlfriend worked in a hospital before. Now she's looking for a part-time job as a secretary.

c. ___ Ming's sister is looking for a job too, but she doesn't have any experience. Also, she can't work after 3:00 because her kids come home from school at 3:30.

d. ___ Ron wants a full-time job as a waiter.

e. ___ Marty's friend Helen wants to quit her job at Q, L & L. She has a degree in accounting.

f. ___ Marty's friend Pedro wants a job in an office. He types very well, but he doesn't want to work after 4:30. He goes to school at night.

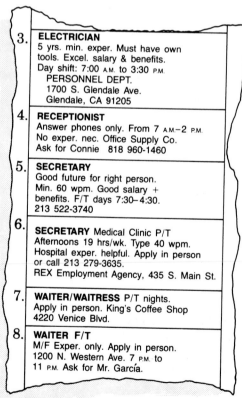

3. **ELECTRICIAN**
5 yrs. min. exper. Must have own tools. Excel. salary & benefits. Day shift: 7:00 A.M. to 3:30 P.M.
PERSONNEL DEPT.
1700 S. Glendale Ave.
Glendale, CA 91205

4. **RECEPTIONIST**
Answer phones only. From 7 A.M.–2 P.M. No exper. nec. Office Supply Co. Ask for Connie 818 960-1460

5. **SECRETARY**
Good future for right person. Min. 60 wpm. Good salary + benefits. F/T days 7:30–4:30.
213 522-3740

6. **SECRETARY** Medical Clinic P/T
Afternoons 19 hrs/wk. Type 40 wpm. Hospital exper. helpful. Apply in person or call 213 279-3635.
REX Employment Agency, 435 S. Main St.

7. **WAITER/WAITRESS** P/T nights.
Apply in person. King's Coffee Shop
4220 Venice Blvd.

8. **WAITER F/T**
M/F Exper. only. Apply in person. 1200 N. Western Ave. 7 P.M. to 11 P.M. Ask for Mr. García.

1. **ACCOUNTANT**
F/T position. No exper. nec. Must be good w/ numbers. Call 213 641-1763

2. **AUTO MECHANIC**
Exper. only. Paid vac. & holidays. Good opportunity for right person. Hank Chang LOS ANGELES MOTORS
6500 Hlwd Blvd. 213 465-9000

Now make a suggestion for each person like this:
Ming should answer the *third* ad because *he wants a job as an electrician.*

For Your Information

Applying for work

You usually apply for a job in person. *In person* means you go to the place. But sometimes it's a good idea to call for more information or to make an appointment first.

Look back at Exercise 2. In the first ad, you have to call because there is no address. But in the second ad, you can go to the place and apply in person, or you can call for more information first.

What about the other ads?

3 Pretend you're looking for a job. Tell a classmate what kind of job you'd like.

A: I'm going to look for a (new) job.
B: Really? What kind of job are you going to look for?
A: I'd like to get a job as *a secretary.*   OR   I'd like to work *in an office.*
B: Do you have any experience?
A: I worked *as a secretary in Laos.*   OR   No, I don't.

4 Ron is talking to Mr. García about a job. Listen and choose the correct answers.

1. In Houston Ron worked as
    a. a waiter part time.
    b. a waiter full time.
    c. Ron didn't say.

2. When Ron was in high school
    a. he worked in a coffee shop.
    b. he didn't work.
    c. He didn't say.

3. Ron likes to work in restaurants because
    a. he likes to clean tables and work in a kitchen.
    b. he likes to talk to people and help them.
    c. He didn't say.

4. Ron
    a. got a job in Mr. García's restaurant.
    b. didn't get a job in his restaurant.
    c. You can't tell from the conversation.

5 Look at the employment application and ask questions about Ron's work experience.

1. Ask about Ron's first job.
    a. Where was Ron's first job?
    b. What was his supervisor's name there?
    c. What kind of work did he do?

    d. How much did he earn?
    e. Why did he quit his job?
2. Ask about his second job.
3. Ask about his most recent job.

APPLICATION FOR EMPLOYMENT

PERSONAL INFORMATION

NAME _Wolinski Ronald J._   SOCIAL SECURITY NO. _047-34-8404_
　　　　Last　　First　　Middle
ADDRESS _152 Franklin Ave.　Los Angeles　CA　90027_
　　　　　Street　　　　City　　　　State　　Zip
TELEPHONE _(213) 350-3817_   REFERRED BY _Marta Cruz_

EDUCATION	Name and Location of School	From	To
Elementary School	Davy Crockett School Freeport Rd., Houston	1969	1977
High School	Stephen Austin H.S. Liberty St., Houston	1977	1981
College, Business or Vocational School	Houston Community College 1210 Oaks Lane, Houston	1981	1983

Position desired _WAITER_
Skills you can use on the job (languages, business machines, etc.) _I speak Polish._
Other activities (sports, hobbies, etc.) _I play the guitar._

WORK EXPERIENCE: List present and past employment. Begin with your most recent employer.

Name and Address of Company	From Mo. Yr.	To Mo. Yr.	Describe your work.	Salary	Reason for leaving	Name of Supervisor
RICK'S CAFE 4702 Westheimer Rd. Houston, Tx Telephone (713) 620-6181	10/84	8/88	I was a waiter part time at night.	$5.00/hr. plus tips	I moved to L.A.	Mrs. Judith Carlson
CINEMA II 4002 Montrose Blvd. Houston, Tx Telephone (713) 367-9155	8/81	10/84	Sometimes I sold tickets, and sometimes I was an usher	$175/wk.	I started acting classes.	Mr. Alan Ramos
HOLIDAY INN COFFEE SHOP 8701 S. Main St. Houston, Tx Telephone (713) 797-1110	9/79	7/81	I cleaned tables and worked in the kitchen.	$3.00/hr.	I got a full-time job.	Mr. Paul Wilks

The information in this application is correct to the best of my knowledge.

SIGNATURE _Ronald J. Wolinski_   DATE _October 3, 1988_

**6 Look at the employment application on page 105.
Then fill out this application for yourself.**

APPLICATION FOR EMPLOYMENT

PERSONAL INFORMATION

NAME _____   SOCIAL SECURITY NO. _____
          Last   First   Middle

ADDRESS _____
          Street   City   State   Zip

TELEPHONE _____   REFERRED BY _____

EDUCATION	Name and Location of School	From	To
Elementary School			
High School			
College, Business or Vocational School			

Position desired _____
Skills you can use on the job (languages,
business machines, etc.) _____
Other activities (sports, hobbies, etc.) _____

WORK EXPERIENCE: List present and past employment. Begin with your most
recent employer.

Name and Address of Company	From Mo. Yr.	To Mo. Yr.	Describe your work.	Salary	Reason for leaving	Name of Supervisor
Telephone						
Telephone						
Telephone						

The information in this application is correct to the best of my knowledge.

SIGNATURE _____   DATE _____

ON YOUR OWN

Do one of the following:

1 Roleplay: Turn to the conversation on
page 98. You are talking to a friend about
your job search. Practice the conversation.

2 Improvise: Work with two classmates.
Change the conversation on page 98. Then
present your conversation to the class.

For pronunciation exercises for Unit 12, see page 112.

REVIEW 6

1 Complete these sentences. Use one of the adverbs in the box. Use each adverb once.

always	sometimes
usually	hardly ever
often	never

1. I _usually_ get up at 8:00, but on Sundays I get up at 10:00.
2. Marty's _____ late. She's never on time.
3. I _____ drive to work. I don't have a car.
4. I _____ see my old boyfriend. I saw him only one time in the last five years.
5. She usually drinks coffee, but _____ she drinks tea. She likes them both.
6. I _____ go to the movies on the weekend. I see about two or three movies a month.

2 Make sentences with these words.

1. I   never   late   am   .

I am never late.

2. usually   She   to   work   drives   .
3. drink   hardly ever   coffee   You   .
4. on time   you   Are   usually   ?
5. he   late   Does   come   sometimes   ?
6. walk   We   to   often   school   .

3 Match the questions in column A with the responses in column B. Complete the questions with an appropriate verb.

A

1. _b_ When did you _get up_ today?
2. ____ Where did you _____ breakfast?
3. ____ What did you _____ ?
4. ____ Why did you _____ your jacket?
5. ____ Did you _____ the newspaper?

B

a. Yes.
b. At 6:30 A.M.
c. I was cold.
d. At home.
e. Orange juice and coffee.

4 Write questions. Begin with _where, when, why_ or _what_.

1. A: _Where did you grow up_ ?
   B: I grew up in New York.
2. A: _____ ?
   B: I went to school there.
3. A: _____ ?
   B: I moved because I wanted to live near my son.
4. A: _____ ?
   B: I came here in 1986.
5. A: _____ ?
   B: In 1987, I went back to school.
6. A: _____ ?
   B: I wanted to learn more English.
7. A: _____ ?
   B: I met my friend at a party.
8. A: _____ ?
   B: He (She) was a part-time student.

5 Marty and Jeff are talking. Complete their conversation. Use *be going to* and the verb in parentheses. Also complete the short answers.

MARTY: *Are* you *going to do* your homework, Jeff?
1. do

JEFF: Yes, I _____ . But first I _____ TV.
2   3. watch

MARTY: No, you _____ TV. You _____ your homework now.
4. watch-*neg.*   5. do

JEFF: Oh, OK. But tonight I _____ my friend David. Is that OK?
6. see

MARTY: That's fine. _____ you _____ dinner at his house?
7. have

JEFF: No, I _____ . Can he have dinner here?
8

MARTY: Sure. I _____ home, but Grandma and Grandpa _____ dinner, and
9. be-*neg.*   10. make

you can eat with them.

6 Make questions with *be going to.* Then answer them with your own information.

1. When/you/do your homework
When are you going to do your homework

2. What/you/do after class
3. Where/you/eat dinner

4. Who/you/eat dinner with
5. What/you/do tomorrow
6. How/you/continue studying English

Just for Fun

7 Complete this crossword puzzle.

Across

1. _____ careful!
2. _____ was your day?
5. Hello.
7. 100% of the time
9. Did you find a job _____ ?
10. Ron's new neighbor
13. Plural of *man*
15. I have a _____ throat.
16. Jeff is Marty's _____ .
17. We see with our _____ .
19. Did you read this job _____ ?
20. Past of *ride*

Down

1. Arms and legs are parts of the _____ .
3. Question for *because*
4. What's the _____ with Jeff?
6. What time _____ it?
8. Words per minute (*abbreviation*)
11. It's a small world, isn't _____ ?
12. Be _____ to (*future*)
13. Ron _____ to a new apartment.
14. Opposite of 7 across
18. _____ , what's new with you?

Pronunciation _____

The Pronunciation exercises are recorded on cassette after the listening exercises for each unit. The Tapescripts are found at the back of the Teacher's Manual.

UNIT 1

Part 1 _____

A. Listen. Which word do you hear—*a.* or *b.?*

1. a. what's   b. what
2. a. name   b. name's
3. a. he's   b. he
4. a. she's   b. she
5. a. where's   b. where

Now listen again and repeat each word.

B. Listen and repeat these sentences.

1. My name's Chris.   3. She's from Los Angeles.
2. Where's she from?

Part 2 _____

Listen and write the contraction you hear.

1. _____ American.   4. My _____ Jim.
2. _____ in class.   5. _____ his name?
3. _____ here.

Now listen again and repeat each sentence.

Part 3 _____

When you ask a *wh-* question,* your voice usually goes down at the end. Listen.

Where are you from?

When you make a statement, your voice goes down at the end too. Listen.

I'm from Texas.

Now listen and repeat these questions and answers.

1. Where's she from?   —She's from New York.
2. What's your last name?   —McCann.
3. How are you?   —I'm fine.

UNIT 2

Part 1 _____

A. Listen and repeat these words.

1. this   5. brother   8. thing
2. these   6. three   9. thanks
3. their   7. thin   10. thick
4. father

B. Listen and repeat these sentences.

1. They're brothers.
2. Please thank them.
3. This is their bathroom.
4. Those are my three brothers.
5. That's my mother.
6. They're not doing anything.

Part 2 _____

Listen. Which sentence do you hear—*a.* or *b.?*

1. a. What's she doing?
   b. What's he doing?
2. a. What's your name?
   b. What's their name?
3. a. Nice to meet you.
   b. It's nice to meet you.
4. a. She's going to L.A.
   b. She's not going to L.A.

Now listen again and repeat each sentence.

Part 3 _____

Listen and repeat these *wh-* questions and answers. Remember that your voice goes down at the end.

1. Where's she going?   –Los Angeles.
2. What's her name?   –Marty Cruz.
3. Where are you from?   –San Francisco.
4. Who's that?   –That's my sister.
5. What's she doing?   –She's reading a newspaper.

---

*A *wh-* question is a question that begins with *who, what, when, where, why* or *how.*

UNIT 3

Part 1

A. Listen. Which word do you hear—a. or b.?

1. a. weigh b. wait   5. a. knee b. neat
2. a. fly   b. flight   6. a. tire b. tired
3. a. pa   b. pop   7. a. lay   b. late
4. a. my   b. Mike

Now listen again and repeat each word.

B. Listen and repeat these sentences.

1. Mike and Bob are neat.
2. My flight is late.
3. Pop is tired tonight.

Part 2

Listen. Which sentence do you hear—a. or b.?

1. a. They're going now.
   b. They aren't going now.
2. a. He isn't an American.
   b. He's an American.
3. a. She's a teacher.
   b. She isn't a teacher.
4. a. We're from Mexico.
   b. We aren't from Mexico.
5. a. You're a student.
   b. You aren't a student.

Now listen again and repeat each sentence.

Part 3

When you ask a _yes/no_ question,* your voice goes up at the end. Listen.

Are you Ron?

Remember—when you make a statement, your voice goes down at the end. Listen.

Yes, I am.

Now listen and repeat these questions and answers.

1. Are you from Laos?   —Yes, I am.
2. Is his name Ron?   —Yes, it is.
3. Are they Americans?   —No, they aren't.
4. Are you going to Chicago?   —Yes, we are.

---

*A _yes/no_ question is a question you answer with _yes_ or _no_.

UNIT 4

Part 1

A. Listen to these words. Which final sound do you hear—_s_ or _z_?

Example: thanks   (s)   z

1.	s	z	5.	s	z
2.	s	z	6.	s	z
3.	s	z	7.	s	z
4.	s	z	8.	s	z

B. Now listen and repeat these words.

1. name's   6. Laos
2. he's   7. it's
3. she's   8. Chris
4. Lyons   9. what's
5. his   10. yes

C. Listen and repeat these sentences.

1. My name's Marty.
2. I'm from Los Angeles.
3. She's Chris.
4. She can speak four languages.

Part 2

A. Listen to the words _can_ and _can't_ in these sentences.

1. I can go.   I can't go.
2. She can speak Spanish. She can't speak French.
3. They can play football. They can't play tennis.

Now listen again and repeat the sentences.

B. Listen and complete the sentences with _can_ or _can't_.

1. She _____ go home.
2. Mike _____ sew.
3. Susan _____ swim.

Now listen again and repeat the sentences.

UNIT 5

Part 1

A. Listen. Which word do you hear—a. or b.?

1. a. wash   b. watch   4. a. shin   b. chin
2. a. dish   b. ditch   5. a. shoes b. choose
3. a. cash   b. catch   6. a. shop   b. chop

Now listen again and repeat each word.

B. Listen and repeat these sentences.

1. How much are the shoes in the shop?
2. Wash the dishes, please.
3. Make sure you watch the children.

C. Listen to these words. Which sound is in the underlined letters—*sh* or *ch?*

1. conver*sa*tion
2. ques*ti*on
3. sta*ti*on
4. vaca*ti*on
5. electri*ci*an
6. sta*tue*
7. recep*ti*onist

Now listen again and repeat each word.

Part 2

Listen and complete the sentences with the pronouns you hear.

1. _____'s an accountant.
2. Where are _____ from?
3. _____'s an actor.
4. Who is _____?

Now listen again and repeat each sentence.

UNIT 6

Part 1

A. Listen. Which word do you hear—*a.* or *b.?*

1. a. jet   b. yet
2. a. joke   b. yolk
3. a. jam   b. yam
4. a. jail   b. Yale

Now listen again and repeat each word.

B. Listen and repeat these sentences.

1. Jack wasn't in jail. He was at Yale.
2. Your jacket isn't here yet.
3. Jane just said yes.

Part 2

Listen and complete these sentences with *was* or *wasn't.*

1. Marty _____ on vacation. She _____ home.
2. I _____ here last year.
3. Jim _____ in Phoenix last week.
4. The weather _____ good.
5. _____ he home?

Now listen again and repeat the sentences.

Part 3

When we speak quickly, we connect many words, and we shorten some vowels. Listen to these sentences.

1. Let's go get a cup of coffee.
2. I'd like a piece of cake and a glass of milk.
3. Can I have a slice of pizza?

Now listen again and repeat the sentences.

UNIT 7

Part 1

A. Listen. Which word do you hear—*a.* or *b.?*

1. a. honey   b. funny
2. a. hair   b. fair
3. a. hail   b. fail
4. a. hound   b. found
5. a. hall   b. fall

Now listen again and repeat each word.

B. Listen and repeat these sentences.

1. Who has fair hair?
2. I found the hound.
3. How's the honey?
4. The house is awful.

Part 2

Listen and repeat these sentences.

1. He doesn't want a car.
2. They don't need books.
3. Does he like hot dogs?   —No, he doesn't.

UNIT 8

Part 1

A. Listen. Which word do you hear—*a.* or *b.?*

1. a. light   b. right
2. a. lime   b. rhyme
3. a. lock   b. rock
4. a. collect b. correct
5. a. lute   b. route
6. a. low   b. row
7. a. lap   b. rap

Now listen again and repeat each word.

B. Listen and repeat these sentences.

1. Repeat the right words.
2. Laura likes Rick.
3. She lives on Regent Road.

Part 2

Listen and complete the sentences with *you, me, him, her* or *them.*

1. I like _____ .
2. She likes _____ .
3. They like _____ .
4. He likes _____ .
5. We like _____ .

Now listen again and repeat the sentences.

UNIT 9

Part 1

A. Listen and repeat these words.

1. study
2. student
3. stay
4. still
5. star
6. strong
7. street
8. strike
9. strange
10. straight

B. Listen and repeat these sentences.

1. You can buy stamps at the store.
2. The students are at the State Street station.
3. They're still on strike.

Part 2

Listen and complete the sentences with *do* or *does* + *you, he, she, we* or *they.*

1. _____ like your English class?
2. _____ work?
3. When _____ get up?
4. Where _____ work?
5. What _____ have to do?

Now listen again and repeat the sentences.

UNIT 10

Part 1

A. Listen and repeat these words.

1. ask
2. desk
3. mask
4. gift
5. soft
6. left
7. last
8. first
9. just
10. object
11. correct
12. looked

B. Listen and repeat these sentences.

1. Dan just left.
2. Her gift is on the desk.
3. Ask for the first one.
4. We have to correct the last sentence.

Part 2

Listen to the word *have* in these two sentences.

I have to go.   I have a book.

Now listen to these sentences and write *have* or *have to.*

1. We _____ a test.
2. They _____ study.
3. I _____ work on Sunday.
4. You _____ class today.

Now listen again and repeat the sentences.

UNIT 11

Part 1

A. Listen and repeat these words.

1. speak
2. Spanish
3. spell
4. sport
5. ski
6. skin
7. sky
8. skirt
9. small
10. smart
11. smell
12. smile

B. Listen and repeat these sentences.

1. I speak Spanish.
2. Skiing and skating are sports.
3. She smells smoke.

Part 2

Listen and complete these sentences with the pronouns and the form of the verb you hear.

1. _____ English.
2. _____ a car.
3. _____ in Japan.
4. _____ baseball.

Now listen again and repeat the sentences.

UNIT 12

Part 1

A. Listen. Which word do you hear—*a.* or *b.?*

1. a. glass   b. grass
2. a. climb   b. crime
3. a. blondes   b. bronze
4. a. flute   b. fruit
5. a. play   b. pray

Now listen again and repeat each word.

B. Listen and write the sentences you hear.

1. _____
2. _____

Now listen again and repeat the sentences.

Part 2

Listen and repeat these sentences.

1. Are we going to go?
2. What time is she going to leave?
3. I'm going to see her tonight.
4. Where is Beth going to be?

Irregular Verbs

Verb	Past Tense		Verb	Past Tense
be	was, were		lie	lay
beat	beat		light	lit *or* lighted
become	became		lose	lost
begin	began		make	made
bend	bent		mean	meant
bet	bet		meet	met
bite	bit		pay	paid
bleed	bled		put	put
blow	blew		read	read
break	broke		ride	rode
bring	brought		ring	rang
build	built		rise	rose
burst	burst		run	ran
buy	bought		say	said
catch	caught		see	saw
choose	chose		sell	sold
come	came		send	sent
cost	cost		set	set
cut	cut		shake	shook
dive	dove		shoot	shot
do	did		shut	shut
draw	drew		sing	sang
drink	drank		sink	sank
drive	drove		sit	sat
eat	ate		sleep	slept
fall	fell		slide	slid
feed	fed		speak	spoke
feel	felt		spend	spent
find	found		spit	spat *or* spit
fly	flew		spread	spread
forget	forgot		stand	stood
forgive	forgave		steal	stole
freeze	froze		stick	stuck
get	got		sting	stung
give	gave		stink	stank *or* stunk
go	went		sweep	swept
grow	grew		swim	swam
have	had		swing	swung
hear	heard		take	took
hide	hid		teach	taught
hit	hit		tear	tore
hold	held		tell	told
hurt	hurt		think	thought
keep	kept		throw	threw
know	knew		understand	understood
lay	laid		wake	woke
lead	led		wear	wore
leave	left		win	won
lend	lent		write	wrote
let	let			

Useful Vocabulary

The Family

Male	Female	Plural
grandfather	grandmother	grandparents
father	mother	parents
son	daughter	children
grandson	granddaughter	grandchildren
brother	sister	brothers and sisters
uncle	aunt	uncles and aunts
nephew	niece	nieces and nephews
cousin	cousin	cousins
husband	wife	
father-in-law	mother-in-law	

Colors

black	brown
white	orange
red	purple
green	pink
blue	gray
yellow	beige

Talking about the weather

Adjectives	Verbs	Nouns
cloudy	blow	breeze
cold	hail	cloud
cool	rain	fog
dry	shine	frost
foggy	sleet	hail
hot	snow	rain
humid		shower
nice		sleet
rainy		snow
sunny		storm
warm		sun
windy		wind

The fifty states and their abbreviations

Alabama	AL	Indiana	IN	Nebraska	NE	South Carolina	SC
Alaska	AK	Iowa	IA	Nevada	NV	South Dakota	SD
Arizona	AZ	Kansas	KS	New Hampshire	NH	Tennessee	TN
Arkansas	AR	Kentucky	KY	New Jersey	NJ	Texas	TX
California	CA	Louisiana	LA	New Mexico	NM	Utah	UT
Colorado	CO	Maine	ME	New York	NY	Vermont	VT
Connecticut	CT	Maryland	MD	North Carolina	NC	Virginia	VA
Delaware	DE	Massachusetts	MA	North Dakota	ND	Washington	WA
Florida	FL	Michigan	MI	Ohio	OH	West Virginia	WV
Georgia	GA	Minnesota	MN	Oklahoma	OK	Wisconsin	WI
Hawaii	HI	Mississippi	MS	Oregon	OR	Wyoming	WY
Idaho	ID	Missouri	MO	Pennsylvania	PA		
Illinois	IL	Montana	MT	Rhode Island	RI		

Occupations

accountant
actor, actress
announcer
architect
artist
baker
bank manager
bank teller
barber
bookkeeper
bricklayer
bus driver
butcher
carpenter
cashier
clerk (general office)
composer
computer operator
computer programmer
construction worker
cook
counselor
dancer
dental hygienist

dentist
designer
doctor
economist
editor
electrician
engineer
factory worker
farmer
file clerk
firefighter
flight attendant
florist
geologist
hairdresser
homemaker
hotel clerk
hotel manager
housekeeper
insurance agent
jeweler
key-punch operator
lawyer
librarian

machine operator
maid
mail carrier
maintenance worker
mathematician
mechanic
minister
model
musician
nurse
optometrist
painter
pharmacist
physical therapist
pilot
plumber
police officer
politician
postal clerk
priest
printer
psychologist
rabbi
receptionist

repairer
reporter
sales clerk
salesperson
scientist
secretary
security guard
shipping clerk
singer
social worker
tailor
taxi driver
teacher
telephone operator
ticket agent
truck driver
typist
veterinarian
waiter, waitress
welder
writer

Stores and Services

Stores

bakery
bookstore
butcher shop
camera store
clothing store
delicatessen
department store
discount store
drugstore
fish market
fruit and vegetable store
furniture store
grocery store
jewelry store
record store
shoe store
stationery store
supermarket
video store

Services

bank
barber
dry cleaner
garage
gas station
hairdresser
laundromat
radio and television
    repair
shoe repair
tailor

Countries	Nationalities	Languages
Argentina	Argentinian	Spanish
Australia	Australian	English
Austria	Austrian	German
Belgium	Belgian	Flemish, Dutch, French
Bolivia	Bolivian	Spanish
Brazil	Brazilian	Portuguese
Canada	Canadian	English, French
Chile	Chilean	Spanish
China	Chinese	Chinese
Colombia	Colombian	Spanish
Costa Rica	Costa Rican	Spanish
Cuba	Cuban	Spanish
Czechoslovakia	Czech	Czech, Slovak
Denmark	Danish	Danish
The Dominican Republic	Dominican	Spanish
Ecuador	Ecuadorean	Spanish
Egypt	Egyptian	Arabic
El Salvador	Salvadorean	Spanish
England	English	English
Finland	Finnish	Finnish, Swedish
France	French	French
Germany	German	German
Great Britain	British	English
Greece	Greek	Greek
Guatemala	Guatemalan	Spanish
Haiti	Haitian	French
Honduras	Honduran	Spanish
India	Indian	Hindi, English
Indonesia	Indonesian	Bahasa Indonesian
Iran	Iranian	Persian
Iraq	Iraqi	Arabic
Israel	Israeli	Hebrew, Arabic
Italy	Italian	Italian
Japan	Japanese	Japanese
Jordan	Jordanian	Arabic
Korea	Korean	Korean
Laos	Laotian	Lao
Lebanon	Lebanese	Arabic
Mexico	Mexican	Spanish
The Netherlands	Dutch	Dutch
Nicaragua	Nicaraguan	Spanish
Nigeria	Nigerian	English
Norway	Norwegian	Norwegian
Pakistan	Pakistani	Urdu, Punjabi, English
Panama	Panamanian	Spanish
Peru	Peruvian	Spanish
The Philippines	Filipino	Pilipino, English, Spanish
Poland	Polish	Polish
Portugal	Portuguese	Portuguese
Saudi Arabia	Saudi Arabian	Arabic
The Soviet Union	Soviet or Russian	Russian
Spain	Spanish	Spanish
Sweden	Swedish	Swedish
Switzerland	Swiss	French, German, Italian
Syria	Syrian	Arabic
Thailand	Thai	Thai
Turkey	Turkish	Turkish
Uruguay	Uruguayan	Spanish
Venezuela	Venezuelan	Spanish
Vietnam	Vietnamese	Vietnamese
Yugoslavia	Yugoslavian	Serbo-Croatian, Slovenian, Macedonian

Word List

The numbers after each word indicate the page number where the word first appears. An asterisk (*) indicates the word is intended for recognition only on that page.

adj = adjective; *adv* = adverb; *aux* = auxiliary verb; *C* = on cassette; *interj* = interjection; *n* = noun; *obj* = object; *pl* = plural; *prep* = preposition; *pron* = pronoun; *s past* = simple past tense; *subj* = subject; *v* = verb

A

a *7, 11
A.M. 68
about 2
    how about? *82C
accent *n* 66
accountant 38
accounting *n* 103
across from 39
acting *n* 93
activity *105
actor 36
actress 37
ad (= advertisement) 98
address *n* 33
admission 68
adult *n* 68
advance: in advance 36
advertising agency 90
aerogram *77
after *prep* 81
    after all 81
    stay after 92
afternoon 21
again 26
agency 98
    advertising agency 90
    employment agency 99
ahead: go ahead* 14C
air conditioning 60
airmail 78
airplane *42
airport 20
all *adj* 48
    adv 44
    all right *7C, 79
    all set *7C
    pron 18
    after all 81
    at all 66
almost 72
alone 59
along: get along (with someone) 93
also *75
always 90
am (be) 1
ambulance *35

American *6
an 27
and 1
ankle 95
another 102
answer *v* 98
any *adj* 11
anything 13
    anything else? 79
anywhere 12
apartment *43, 56
    apartment building *63
apple 27
appliance *73
application *82C
apply 103
are (be) 2
area
    area code 35
    dining area 54
arm *n* (part of the body) 95
around here 75
arrive 20
ask *86
asleep 21
aspirin 96
at *7, 13
attic 57
auditorium *69C
aunt 81
avenue 32

B

baby 100
back *adv* 12
    n (part of the body) 95
    go back 12
backache 95
backpack 26
bad 8
    not too bad 8
bag 26
bakery 72
balcony 58
bank *n* 64
baseball 48

basement 57
basketball 67
bathroom 54
battery 72
be *19
    am 1
    are 2
    is 1
    was 45
    were 45
    be born 93
beach 21
beautiful 44
because 90
become 102
bed: in bed 97
bedroom 54
beef: roast beef 50
before *prep* 81
begin 81
    began 93
behind 72
benefits *103
best 62
between 39
big 54
bike *n* 91
birthday *42, 43
birthplace *68
bite: a bite to eat 51
black 44
blade: razor blade 96
blank *adj* 74
blouse 27
blue 27
boarding pass *7C
book *n* *7, 26
bookstore 73
boring *adj* 48
born: be born 93
borrow 36
boss *n* 63
bottle of 96
boulevard 32
bowling: go bowling *82
box of 96
boy 11
boyfriend 11
brand *n* (= type) *73

break: give me a break! *n* 90
breakfast *92
breathe 96
bring 80
broke (= without money) 98
brother 10
brown 27
building 55
    apartment building *63
bus 13
    bus station 18
business 86
    business machine *105
busy 80
but 26
buy 81
    bought *s past* 84
by train/truck/ship *77
bye 26
bye-bye 33

C

café *105
cafeteria 73
cake 50
call *v* *69C, 85
    phone call 40
can *v* 9
candy bar 41
cannot 29
car 28
    car make *43
    car model *43
card 32
    identification card 27
care: take care of *92
carpet 60
cassette 13
    cassette player 27
cent 41
center: information center *68
Centigrade *47
chair 55
chalk 27

may (permission) *86C, 87
maybe 72
me *7, 19
medicine 90
    cough medicine 96
meet 8
    met s past 93
memorial 68
mention v
    don't mention it *43C, 72
menu *50
message 86
    take a message 86
middle *6
midnight 62
milk 44
milkshake 50
million *68
mine pron 26
minimum 103
minute n 26
Miss 6
miss v 62
model: car model *43
modern 55
mom 18
money 26
month 42
moon *42
morning 19
    good morning 1
mother 11
mouth 95
move v (one's residence) 93
    move in 80
movie 21
Mr. 6
Mrs. 6
Ms. 6
much
    how much? 32
    thank you very much 24
music 67
    popular music 67
musical 30
musician 36
my 1
mystery 67

N

name n 1
nap: take a nap 97
nasal spray 96
nationality *6
near 39
nearby *74, 75
necessary 103
neck 95
need v 57
    need to 58

neighbor 55
neighborhood 55
never 90
new 54
    what's new? 90
news 67
newspaper 19
next *14C, 20
    you're next 62
next to 72
nice *7C, 8
    it's nice to meet you 8
nickel 41
nickname 8
night 48
    night school *93
    tomorrow night 20
nightlife 66
no 11
nobody *84
noise 66
noisy 55
noon *47, 62
north 32
nose 95
not 3
    not too bad 8
notebook 26
nothing 51
now *7, 13
    right now 13
number n 26
    be good with numbers *103
    emergency number *31
    social security number *105
    telephone number 26
nurse n 37

O

o'clock 18
occupation *43
of 7
off
    cross off *99
    day off *85
office 39
    office manager 102
    post office 72
officer *14C
often 91
oh 3
OK *7C, 8
    that's OK 98
old 55
    how old? 90
Olympics *68
on *7, 19
one pron *58, 72
only 60

open adj 68
    v *7
operator: telephone operator 33
opinion *55C, 58
opportunity *103
opposite 56
or 21
orange adj 27
    n 27
order: side order *50
originally 62
other adj *31
our 9
out
    fill out 32
    find out 85
    go out to eat 85
    over and out *14C
over adv 22
    over and out *14C
overtime *92, 102
own adj 58

P

P.M. 68
pack of 41
package 77
    package of 96
page *7
paid adj *103
paint v 30
paper *7
parcel post *78
pardon? 72
parent 10
part n 60
part-time 93
passenger 18
past: half past 25
patio 58
pay v 60
    it pays well 92
pen 26
pencil 26
penny 41
people 13
per
    hours per week 103
    words per minute 103
perfect adj *48
period *33
person: in person 103
personal *105
personnel *103
phone n 31
    phone call 40
piano 30
pick up 20
pie 50
piece *7
    piece of 27

pizza 51
place n *64
    place of employment *64
play n *73
    v 26
player: cassette player 27
please *7, 15
plus 60
police n *31
    police officer 37
pollution 66
pool 57
    swimming pool 75
porch 57
position (= job) 102
post
    parcel post *78
    post office 72
postcard 77
pot of *92
practice n 83
present v *69C
president *42
pretty adv 8
price n *69C, *73
print v *6
probably 74
processing
    data processing 86
    word processing 86
program n 67
proud *69C
purse 27
put *33

Q

quarter 41
    a quarter after 25
    a quarter to 25
question n *101
quiet 55
quit 101

R

racket: tennis racket 28
rain v 84
rainy 47
raise n 102
rated adj *69C
razor blade 96
read *7, 13
    read s past 83
ready 18
real adv 80
really 66
    really? *43C, 104
recent *105
receptionist 38
record n 73

tour *n* *68, 85
town 40
traffic 66
train *n* *77
transportation 60
treat: my treat 44
trip *n* 100
truck *77, 99
try 72
tube of 96
tuna fish 50
TV 13
type *v* 30

U

ugly 55
uh-huh *43C
umbrella 27
uncle 81
uncomfortable 55
under 68
understand 15
   I don't understand 15
unfortunately *74
unfriendly 55
unfurnished 60
up
   get up 83
   grow up 93
   pick up 20
upstairs 39
us 63
usher *n* 105
usually *77, 91

utilities 60

V

vacation 44
   on vacation *44
vanilla 50
vegetable 75
very 18
vice president 102
video *73
view *n* 54
violin 30
visit *v* 81
visitor *68
vocational school *105

W

wait 26
   wait a minute 26
   wait for 13
waiter 93
waitress 38
walk *v* 91
wallet 27
wall-to-wall 60
want *v* 57
   want to 58
warm *adj* 47
was (be) 45
watch *n* 24
   v 13
water *n* 60
we 2
wear 62

weather 44
   weather report *47
week 20
weekend 20
weight *77
welcome: you're welcome 26
well *adv* 26
   (= healthy) 15
   interj 26
were (be) 45
west 32
what? 4
   what about you? 2
   what color is it? 27
   what do you do? 64
   what's new? 90
   what's the date? 36
   what's the matter? 90
what a . . . ! 55
what kind? 36
when? 42
where? 4
which? *96
while: for a while 100
who? 38
whose? 26
why? 90
   why don't you . . . ? 72
wife (*pl* wives) 11
will ('ll) 86
with 20
woman (*pl* women) 38
wonderful 44
word 103
   word processing 86

work *n* 20
   v 98
world *73, 90
   it's a small world 90
worry *v* *55C, 90
   don't worry about it 90
would 15
   I'd like 44
   I'd love to 80
wrist 95
write *7, 13
   write soon 61
wrong 20

Y

yard 57
yeah *7C, 8
year 42
   school year 100
yellow 27
yep *43C
yes 11
yesterday 45
yet 98
   not yet 98
you 2
   you *obj* 4
   you *subj* 2
your 4
yours 28
yourself *104C

Z

zip code 33

Acknowledgements

We wish to thank the following for providing us with photographs:

Page 3, *left to right:* Courtesy of Porsche Cars North America; National Zoological Park, Smithsonian Institution; Courtesy of the Panasonic Company; Courtesy of the American Numismatic Society, New York. **Page 22,** *left to right:* American Airlines, Photo by Bob Takis; United Airlines Photo; Trans World Airlines Photo. **Page 37,** *top row, left to right, pic. 2:* Photo by A. Sue Weisler, Rochester Institute of Technology; *pics. 3 and 4:* Photos by Heinz Paul Piper; *center row, left to right:* Courtesy of Christ Hospital, Jersey City, New Jersey; Barbara Baxley in the Yale Repertory Theatre Production of *Mrs. Warren's Profession,* William B. Carter, Photographer; Courtesy of the New York City Police Department; University of Rochester, Office of Public Relations, Jeff Goldberg, Photographer; *bottom row, left to right:* Reproduced with permission of the AT&T Corporate Archive; University of Rochester, Office of Public Relations, Jeff Goldberg, Photographer. **Page 42,** *top left:* National Air and Space Museum, Smithsonian Institution; *top right:* National Aeronautics and Space Administration; *center left:* Courtesy of the New York Convention and Visitors Bureau; *center right:* National Portrait Gallery, Smithsonian Institution: On loan from Lord Rosebery; *bottom:* Reproduced with permission of AT&T Corporate Archive. **Page 47,** *left to right, pics. 1 and 4:* National Oceanic and Atmospheric Administration; *pic. 2:* Hawaii Visitors Bureau; *pic 3:* Vermont Travel Division. **Page 67,** *pic. 1:* Taro Yamasaki, Photographer; *pic. 2:* Courtesy of Arista Records; *pic. 3:* Courtesy of Bruce Springsteen; *pic. 4:* ©Copyright BLACK BULL MUSIC, INC. 1984; *pic. 6:* Courtesy of Paramount Pictures; *pic. 7:* Courtesy of "Dynasty"; *pic. 8:* Courtesy of Musidor B.V. **Page 68:** Photos courtesy of the Greater Los Angeles Convention and Visitors Bureau. **Page 73:** Burnsville Center, 1.2 million square foot super-regional shopping mall, Burnsville, Minnesota.